THE MIRACLE MOMENT

A Six-Week
Bible Study on
Transforming Conflict
into Connection

NICOLE UNICE

TYNDALE
MOMENTUM®

The Tyndale nonfiction imprint

Visit Tyndale online at tyndale.com.

Visit Tyndale Momentum online at tyndalemomentum.com.

Visit the author at nicoleunice.com.

TYNDALE, Tyndale's quill logo, *Tyndale Momentum*, and the Tyndale Momentum logo are registered trademarks of Tyndale House Ministries. Tyndale Momentum is the nonfiction imprint of Tyndale House Publishers, Carol Stream, Illinois.

The Miracle Moment Participant's Guide: A Six-Week Bible Study on Transforming Conflict into Connection

Designed by Eva M. Winters

Published in association with Jenni Burke of Illuminate Literary Agency: www.illuminateliterary.com.

For information about special discounts for bulk purchases, please contact Tyndale House Publishers at csresponse@tyndale.com, or call 1-855-277-9400.

ISBN 978-1-4964-4860-6

Printed in the United States of America

27 26 25 24 23 22 21
7   6   5   4   3   2   1

Contents

A Word of Welcome

WELCOME, MY FRIEND, to this study of the messy, mundane, and miraculous experience we call life.

If you are struggling with a frustrating, annoying, or *just plain difficult* relationship in your life and you've decided to do something about it . . .

If you've been wondering about that gap between what you desire from your conversations and what you actually experience . . .

If you want to know God better but aren't sure how to take what the Bible says and apply it . . .

You are my people.

My people are those who aren't content to receive information without doing something about it. My people are the ones who wrestle and wonder about their interpersonal interactions while deeply longing for more out of life—more out of themselves, more out of their experience with God, and more out of their relationships.

Whether you found this study because you've read *The Miracle Moment* and you know you need help to implement it . . .

Or you are in a small group at your church or a book club in your neighborhood and you've decided to encourage and support each other in working through the relational transformation promised through *The Miracle Moment* . . .

Or someone just gifted you this workbook and you are wondering *what in the world they meant* when they said they think this could be helpful to you . . .

Then you are in the right place.

I wrote *The Miracle Moment* as a practical guide for handling that one relationship (and we all seem to have at least one) in which we feel defensive, inadequate, or uncomfortable. When conflict occurs, most of us respond as if on cue to an unwritten and repetitive script that typically drives us even further apart. In *The Miracle Moment*, I reveal what I've discovered about how we can flip that script. We begin by acknowledging that every conversation contains a potential "miracle moment." It's not the moment you react to being hurt, misunderstood, or treated unfairly in a relationship. It's the moment *after* the initial reaction, when you change course and respond differently. A moment when you can choose to do the risky work of moving *toward* the other person in your response instead of putting up barriers designed to shut things down.

If you've read that book, you may have noticed that it contains a little less Bible teaching than my previous books. That was intentional: I wanted to be sure you could give the book to any of your friends, coworkers, or neighbors for the straight-up relationship teaching that it provides. But what you are going to experience in the next six weeks is the source of everything in *The Miracle Moment*. Every single truth contained in that book is deeply rooted in Scripture. Every opportunity for meaning what you feel, saying what you mean, and doing what you say comes from God's design for our flourishing as humans.

In this guide, we will dive deeper into the biblical principles that inform healthy relationships. You will discover:

- How Jesus uses our lives as His classroom; this is where He teaches us about healthy relationships
- Why self-awareness is not selfish but required for a God-honoring life
- How to apply the virtues of humility, unity, and forgiveness to difficult relationships
- What healthy boundaries looked like for Jesus—and what that means for us

We are embarking on a journey to understand how God has wired us, renewed us in Christ, and set us free to experience depth and goodness in our relationships. When we ask for Jesus' wisdom to navigate complicated relationships, He will always answer. Our job is to be willing to listen and accept that the only person we have control of is ourselves. That's why the first two sessions center on ways to increase our self-awareness, not how to better relate to other people. Then we'll spend the subsequent sessions on the practical, biblical steps of alignment in our relationships: how to mean what we feel, say what we mean, and do what we say—no matter how challenging the situation.

Remember, Jesus says, "Walk with me and work with me."[1] He expects us to be *in practice*, not *in perfection*, when it comes to the classroom that is our life.

My hope is this: that you might use these next six weeks to discover—or rediscover—how powerful it is to prioritize your relationship with God as the primary and essential relationship in your life. My prayer is this: that you might grasp a little better the depth of God's love for you and His intentional engagement in your ongoing transformation in Christ.

And my promise is this: There is no condemnation in Christ,[2] and there is no condemnation here. Use this study exactly as you need it in this season. If that means you spend five minutes with the meditation moment each day and skip all the homework the first time around—my hope is that you'll come back again and keep learning! If it means you watch the videos and use the assessments—that's fine too. If it means you get acquainted with your Bible and begin to engage with God for the first time on your own—that's a great first step. Take it bite by bite, trusting the Spirit of God to lead you into insight and truth.

Now for those of you who appreciate direction and details, here are a few FAQs and my answers.

1. WHAT DO I NEED TO DO THIS STUDY?

You'll need this study guide, a Bible, and the six video sessions. Here is how each component fits:

- The study guide and videos are designed to be used together. The videos are available in *The Miracle Moment DVD Experience* or via streaming at rightnowmedia.org. In the videos, I teach straight from the Bible so you can apply God's wisdom to your relationship with yourself and others. I also want to help you recognize potential miracle moments right in front of you. The study guide takes these truths and makes them more interactive as we open the Bible together and walk through some life-changing principles.

- If you don't already have it, I recommend that you pick up *The Miracle Moment*. Although it is not required, the book brings color and shape to all the principles of this story. I use stories from my life and my engagements with clients and leaders to paint a picture of what miracle moments can look like in your day-to-day life. It provides personal coaching in the practical steps you can take to experience miracle moments.

You can read *The Miracle Moment* first and reinforce what you've learned through the study, or you can read it as you complete the study. Either way, at the start of each session, you'll be pointed to the chapters from the book that correspond with it.

2. SHOULD I COMPLETE THIS STUDY ON MY OWN OR WITH A GROUP?

The curriculum may be completed either individually or together, in a small or large group setting. You may need or want to work through this material independently, and you can certainly do that. In that case, "being together" will involve a conversation between you and me, you and God, and you and whomever you discover God is using to bring miracle moments into your life.

If you have the opportunity to complete this study with others—whether one friend over coffee, a small group in your living room, or several people in a virtual book club—I recommend that approach.

Hebrews 10:24-25 says, "Let us consider how we may spur one another on toward love and good deeds, not giving up meeting together." I firmly believe that life is hard, and we need all the help we can get. When we share our own journey with honesty and openness, we discover that those around us are often struggling with similar things. When we choose to try courageous new ways of loving people, our group can provide us with the encouragement and confidence to follow through.

Whether you're working through the guide on your own or with a group, I encourage you to access the Choose the Miracle Toolkit. It is located at nicoleunice.com/miracles, and it includes an answer key and resources for a one-week boot camp to help you make the most of your miracle moments.

3. I'D LIKE TO DO THE STUDY IN A GROUP, BUT HOW DO I FIND ONE?

Why not start one? It may be easier than you think. It may just take a simple text to a friend, neighbor, or coworker: "I'm starting a Bible study that focuses on healthy relationships. Want to join?" The worst they can say is no!

Those in the church have often made *witness* a verb, as in "I need to witness to my friend." But in reality, *witness* is a noun. It's a state of being. Each of us is called to be a witness—in our neighborhoods, our work teams, our churches, and any other circle of influence.

Our "witness" is our life lived out together, a life in which we experience miracles—miracles of insight, miracles of connection, and miracles of transformation and love in our relationships. When we observe those miracles in ourselves and others, we develop perseverance to "keep the faith."

4. OK—I'M IN! I'M GOING LEAD A GROUP FOR THE FIRST TIME. CAN YOU HELP?

Whether you're a veteran small group leader or are ready to jump in with some friends and lead a group for the first time, I want to help! Turn to page 145 to access the leader's guide and helpful hints, as well as individual session outlines for each week.

5. IS THIS STUDY APPROPRIATE FOR [WOMEN, MEN, COUPLES, COLLEGE KIDS, NEW BELIEVERS, OLD BELIEVERS, LEADERS]?

Yes, yes, and *yes*! This study will benefit anyone who relates to anyone (and that's everyone—including you!). The material is designed to be accessible and relevant, no matter what stage of life you're in.

6. HOW LONG SHOULD EACH SESSION TAKE TO COMPLETE?

Each group video session is structured so that it can be completed in ninety minutes. You can take longer if needed, but I've found that most people's attention begins to wane at that point. If you have less time, you can discuss fewer questions and move more of the group work to participants' personal study time.

If you are studying on your own, it will take less time to work through the videos (about fifteen to twenty minutes) and the Bible study (about thirty minutes).

In addition, working through this guide involves about fifteen minutes of daily work (five days a week) to help you get into the habit of reading God's Word on a regular basis. If you haven't yet developed the habit of spending time with God, I encourage you to remove one distraction from your day and replace that time with this book's daily work for the duration of the study. There's room to record your reflections right in the participant's guide.

7. WHY ARE SCRIPTURE MEMORIZATION AND MEDITATION PROMPTS INCLUDED IN THIS STUDY?

Scripture is how God speaks to us today, so we don't want to simply read it and forget it. To ensure God's truth sticks with you, I'll invite you to commit to memory a short phrase or verse from Scripture each week. Memorizing passages hard-codes them into the brain so they aren't erased, even when you don't use them for a while. This practice fills the "hard drive" of your brain with promises that can come back to you long after you've done the work to "code" them to memory.[3] By the end of this study, you'll have something priceless that will last long after my words fade.

Each Daily Rhythm ends with a Meditation Moment. Miracle moments don't happen when we avoid actual connection with Christ—even if we gain a lot of head knowledge by studying the Bible! That is why I invite you to spend a significant amount of your daily Bible study time creating space to listen for Christ's voice in your life. We will start with just three to five minutes. If that makes you feel antsy, you can set your cell phone timer so that you can focus exclusively on this time with Christ.

8. WHAT DO ALL THE ICONS WITHIN THE SESSIONS MEAN?

Throughout the sessions, you'll see helpful icons to guide your journey and help you get oriented, whether you are studying on your own or with a group.

Main Point
This introduces the key phrase in each session.

Video
This indicates when to tune in to the video component of the study.

Reflection/Application
This icon indicates opportunities to make time for personal reflection and application, either on your own or during your small group lesson.

In the Word
The book icon tells you when to delve more deeply into the Bible, whether individually or in your group.

Memory Moment
This points to a key verse or phrase from Scripture to commit to memory.

Daily Rhythms
Each session includes five sections for a daily, fifteen- to twenty-minute engagement with what you're learning. This work is designed to help you develop a practice of looking upward (to God) and inward (for personal growth) to open your eyes to your miracle moments.

Meditation Moment
This icon invites you to a time of quiet contemplation with God as

you end each day's study. You might be surprised by how much growth comes from simply learning to be still.

Group
If you are leading a group through the participant's guide and are looking for extra guidance, look for this icon in the leader's guide.

OK, new friend, one more thing—I'd love to hear from you! If you'd like to share how *The Miracle Moment* has impacted your life or group, let me know. You can reach me through social media or at nicoleunice.com.

God has given us a beautiful, abundant vision for what our relationships in Christ can look like. We can tell the entire, honest truth about our own shortcomings. We can experience abundant grace and forgiveness through the power of the Holy Spirit (more on that in week 2!), and most important, we can truly "love one another" because Christ first loved us.[4] Let's jump in!

Much love,
Nicole

SETTING UP FOR A MIRACLE

∧∧∧∧∧

That's the incredible thing about being human:
We are flawed, but we are never finished.
The Miracle Moment, chapter 1, page 14

∧∧∧∧∧

This Week's Recommended Reading:
Chapters 1 and 2 in *The Miracle Moment*

I ONCE HEARD a speaker tell a joke about a frustrated preacher who came to God in prayer and said, "God, I love leading your church. It's just the people I can't stand."

There is no place in which the truth of our transformation in Christ becomes more evident than in our frustrating, difficult, real relationships with one another. Everything we say and believe about Jesus' presence and power in our lives is visible in the way we love others, including (and especially) the relationships that are most challenging. In fact, it's in the relationships that feel the *most* impossible that we are *most* primed for miracles. Let's look at what it takes to be in position to see them.

 To love like Jesus is to believe like Jesus.

 Tune in to video session 1: "Setting Up for a Miracle."

Video Notes

A miracle moment is the moment of transformation where you act in the power of the Spirit to *love differently*.

Perspective is powerful.

The 5 Laws of Miracles:

1.

2.

3.

4.

5.

Are you ready for a miracle?

A Moment of Reflection

1. On your own or with your group, write down one phrase or thought from the video teaching that stands out.

2. In Matthew 11:29 (MSG) Jesus gives this invitation: "Walk with me and work with me." Name two or three relationships or places in your life where you could invite Jesus to be your teacher.

3. Describe a season in your life when your perspective shifted in some way. What were some lessons you learned during that time?

4. I think we all have a relationship (or two or three) that feels impossible to change. If you agree, circle all the reasons that make that feel true:

   a. The person is not interested in changing.

   b. I can't help but be frustrated/anxious/angry in their presence.

   c. We've tried before, and it's never worked.

   d. It doesn't feel like the effort it would take is worth it.

   e. I'm tired of being the only one making an attempt.

In the Word

Let's look at a few Scripture passages that illustrate how God set up the making of miracles in His followers:

1. Read Exodus 3:1-6. What important quality does Moses display that sets him up to experience God's power?

2. Read Luke 5:1-10. What important quality does Simon Peter display that sets him up to experience God's provision?

3. Read Matthew 9:20-22. What important quality does the woman display that sets her up for a miracle?

4. Which character from these passages do you resonate with most? Why?

Application

In this short survey of Scripture, we've discovered that curiosity, openness to try new things, and wild hope are all characteristics of people who have life-changing interactions with God. On a scale of 1 to 10, rate yourself on these three characteristics. (Remember: There is no reason to sugarcoat your answers; this exercise is just for you! This is a great opportunity to explore your perspective as we go into our daily study.)

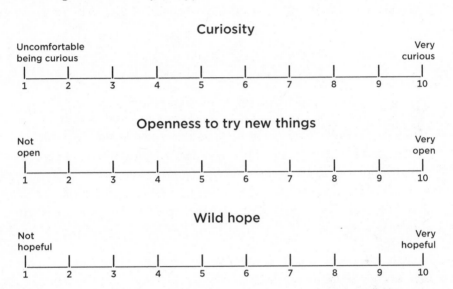

During this week's study, we will lay out the laws of miracles—the fundamental beliefs we can foster that prime us to see the miracle moments around us. We'll spend the following weeks on the practical, biblical steps of alignment in our relationships: how to mean what we feel, say what we mean, and do what we say, no matter how challenging the situation. Remember, Jesus says, "Walk with me and work with me" (Matthew 11:29, MSG). He expects us to be *in practice* not *in perfection* when it comes to the classroom that is our life.

Memory Moment

Because of the Lord's mercy and grace, we have hope that we can grow—both individually and in our relationships. All of this is rooted in our connection with God, made possible by Christ's death on the cross. (We'll consider the basis of our hope more fully on day 5.) With this in mind, let's spend time this week taking in this promise from God:

> I remain confident of this: I will see the goodness of the LORD in the land of the living.
> PSALM 27:13

Closing Prayer

A prayer for you as we embark on this journey together:

> *Jesus, You've told us, "As I have loved you, so you must love one another" (John 13:34). You've given us this impossibly high standard for the way we are to love in relationships—one we will experience only through Your miraculous, powerful love. Open our eyes to experience the depths of Your love for us this week, and give us the desire to invite You in as our teacher every single day.*

Daily Rhythms

During His ministry, Jesus said something haunting to the "religious people": "You study the Scriptures diligently because you think that in them you have eternal life. These are the very Scriptures that testify about me, yet you refuse to come to me to have life" (John 5:39-40).

My prayer for our time is that these studies will not just be a way to "check the box" for having done your Bible study but will become a daily rhythm, a time you set aside to truly come to Christ, the very source of our life.

Day 1: Nice Is Bad

Bible Reading: JOHN 5:1-15

Before we begin a new activity, we want to know what our end goal is. In a world of analytics, we've been trained to ask the question "How will I know if I'm successful?" So for the purposes of our study, I want to offer you a definition. A miracle moment is

> . . . the moment in a conversation when you want to shut up, give up, or blow up—and you lean in instead. It's not the moment you react to being hurt, misunderstood, or treated unfairly. It's the moment after the initial reaction, when you change course and respond differently.
> *THE MIRACLE MOMENT*, PAGE 13

Miracle moments are those small, critical junctures in life when we love differently. In our difficult relationships, it's the second when Holy Spirit–empowered love comes from us, despite us, rather than our normal human reaction of defensiveness, hostility, or withdrawal. In order to love like Jesus, we have to believe like Jesus, which means seeing the world from His perspective. That is where the five laws of miracles come in, those beliefs that enable us to position ourselves for miracle moments:

The Five Laws of Miracles

Law #1: Nice is bad

In love, in work, in life—deep relationships require vulnerability, good fights, and a much more powerful kind of love than being "nice."

Law #2: Chaos before order

We naturally default to many unhelpful behaviors in our relationships—distance instead of depth, blame instead of apologies, and talking about and around each other rather than to each other. To experience freedom in Christ, we have to unlearn these practices, which sometimes feels uncomfortable or awkward.

Law #3: Curious, not condemning

If we shut down the process of discovering why we or those around us act as we do, we cannot learn anything. Nothing shuts down our development faster than self-condemnation.

Law #4: Small is big

Miracle moments result not in a massive, all-at-once transformation, but in small, incremental changes to our way of relating.

Law #5: Hope makes change possible

Your connection to something beyond yourself, your engagement with the world, and your awareness of your part in life's greater story bring hope, which can lead to change.

These laws represent a shift in our perspective on what it means to learn from Jesus through (not despite) our difficult relationships. This week, we'll focus on each of these laws individually, beginning with law #1: Nice is bad.

Turn to John 5. Take a few deep breaths as you bring your attention to the scene in verses 1-15 and imagine watching it happen in front of you.

1. What three words would you use to describe Jesus in this scene?

    a.

    b.

    c.

Perhaps you chose words like *powerful, compassionate, loving, strong, mysterious,* or *patient*. My guess is you did not choose the word *nice*. There is a sense that if I'm a Christian, I must be nice. But when we use that word, we're usually describing someone who backs down or steps away from conflict rather than a person who engages it with love and purpose. Jesus models another way for us—He offers an invitation to experience the fullness of His life differently.

2. If Jesus were to ask you, "Do you want to get well?" in what areas of your life would you be open to His healing and change? (Some possibilities are your anxious or self-critical thoughts; your financial health, marriage, or parenting; or your lack of contentment or joy.)

3. When it comes to the way you handle conflict, if Jesus asked, "Do you want to get well?" how might you respond? Circle all that apply:

I want to be more vulnerable.	I want to be more compassionate.
I need to stand up for my convictions.	I want to follow through with my actions.
I need to learn to apologize.	Other: _____

4. Most of us would not choose *nice* as the word we would want used in our eulogy to describe us. When it comes to how you relate with people, what three words would you like to be used to describe you?

 ## Meditation Moment

We opened our week with these words from Jesus, which He speaks right after He heals the man at the pool.

> You study the Scriptures diligently because you think that in them
> you have eternal life. These are the very Scriptures that testify about
> me, yet you refuse to come to me to have life.
> JOHN 5:39-40

Scripture meditation is a way to come to Christ to listen to His voice. We will start with three to five minutes of meditation each day this week. If this practice is new to you and you feel a bit antsy, you can set a timer on your cell phone or in your kitchen to keep you focused exclusively on Christ for those moments.

I like to use simple phrases to center my heart on the promises of God. Drawing from today's lesson, here's a thought to focus on:

Jesus,
I bring my life
to your life.

You don't need to look for a specific "result" from this time. You are simply engaging in the practice of coming in faith into God's presence. He will do the rest.

Day 2: Chaos before Order

Bible Reading: JOHN 3:1-8

In *Renovation of the Heart,* Dallas Willard says that the enemy of our own growth is the lie that we are okay when "realistically, I'm *not* okay and you're *not* okay. We're all in serious trouble. That must be our starting point."[1] The temptation is to believe that *I'm okay and Jesus makes me better.* The truth, however, is that while we are souls of great worth, we are also hopelessly lost.

Just consider our relationships. We naturally default to many unhelpful behaviors—distance instead of depth, blame instead of apologies, talking about and around each other rather than to each other. We must navigate an uncomfortable season of unlearning these reactions before we can experience true freedom in Christ.

Law #2, then, is *chaos before order.* Demolition comes before renovation. Taking apart comes before rebuilding.

Ask the Holy Spirit to lead you into truth today as we hop around the Gospels to discover how Jesus describes this life with Him.

Read John 3:1-8. Nicodemus comes to Jesus at night, presumably so he could keep his interest in Jesus private. I imagine Nicodemus must have been disturbed, confused, and even astonished at their conversation and the claims Jesus made about what it truly means to follow God.

1. In John 3:3, Jesus gives Nicodemus an answer that dismantles his understanding of religion. Record what Jesus says is required to see God's Kingdom:

2. Now turn to Luke 5:1-11, which we looked at earlier. In verse 10, Jesus gives Peter a new vision for his life. Record Jesus' words here:

3. Read John 6:35. What does Jesus say about Himself, and what does He promise? Record your answer here:

4. Finally, read John 20:21-23. What strange action does Jesus take in this passage?

5. From what you've read today, how would you describe what Jesus is really offering in a relationship with Him? What does that show us about how He wants us to treat one another in relationships?

Before we can recognize miracle moments in our lives, we must relate to God and others in new ways that often demand radical change that feels chaotic and disconcerting.

Meditation Moment

Take the final few minutes of your time today to simply imagine yourself coming to Christ, as Nicodemus did. What Gospel story from the previous two pages resonates with you most? Bring that story to mind and sit quietly with it, inviting Jesus to reveal anything He wants you to know today.

After your quiet time, record below any thoughts or feelings you had as you reflected on that passage.

Day 3: Curious, Not Condemning

Bible Reading: MATTHEW 13:1-17

One of the main recurring refrains in Jesus' teaching was this little phrase: "Whoever has ears, let them hear" (Matthew 13:9). In other words, Jesus said that *hearing is a choice.* Nothing shuts down our development faster than self-condemnation. Curiosity, or openness to Christ's message, is the path to discovery and growth.

Our passage today has two parts: the parable that Jesus tells and His conversation with the disciples afterward.

1. In the parable, Jesus gives three reasons why a seed isn't ultimately fruitful. What are those reasons?

    a.

    b.

    c.

2. Jesus interprets this parable in Luke 8:11-15. What three reasons does He give for the Word being unfruitful in our lives?

    a.

    b.

    c.

3. Finally, turn to Matthew 13:14-15. What reason does Jesus give for why people might not be able to hear or see the truth?

Callousness and condemnation—of ourselves or others—stifles growth in our relationships; curiosity helps them flourish.

Meditation Moment

Psalm 51:10 says, "Create in me a pure heart, O God, and renew a steadfast spirit within me." Take a few moments to invite Christ to move in your heart, and then spend three to five minutes with God reflecting on places your heart might be calloused. Calluses are formed by friction and wear and tear—our bodies form them to protect us. Are there areas where you've been trying to protect your heart because of hurt, fear, worry, or insecurity? Imagine bringing those places into the healing and renewing presence of the Spirit.

Day 4: Small Is Big

Bible Reading: LUKE 6:46-49

Miracle moments exist not in massive, all-at-once transformation but in small, incremental changes to our way of relating. That should be good news if you are feeling as if the bar is too high and the work is impossible. But Jesus simply invites us to be *in practice* with Him. It's in those small changes that you will experience powerful transformation. Let's take a closer look at the small shifts that make a radical difference in our life with God.

1. Read Luke 6:46-49. In verse 48, what three things does Jesus say that people with solid foundations do?

   a.

   b.

   c.

2. Read Matthew 11:28-30. What does Jesus promise will happen to those who come to Him?

   a.

   b.

3. What does Jesus state about His own character that makes it safe for us to come to Him?

4. Read Matthew 9:13. Who does Jesus say He came for?

As the Scriptures above illustrate, Jesus makes huge promises about what He will do in response to the small things we can do (come to Him, listen, practice). Ready for a curveball? **Read Jesus' words in Luke 14:26-27**, remembering the first law of miracles (*nice is bad*):

> If anyone comes to me and does not hate father and mother, wife and children, brothers and sisters—yes, even their own life—such a person cannot be my disciple. And whoever does not carry their cross and follow me cannot be my disciple.

In our first three examples, we experience the humble and gentle heart of Christ, who invites us to come to Him. The only prerequisite is bringing Him our weary, burdened, sinful selves. But Jesus' words in Luke 14 appear critical and harsh at first glance. Here's where context can help. Jesus had just told a story about a king who threw a great banquet, only to learn that his invited guests had refused to come because they were too busy. And in Luke 14:28-32, Jesus asks the people around Him to imagine a builder who doesn't count the cost before beginning construction on a tower and a king who doesn't assess his troops before going to war. Jesus sandwiches His "come to me" command between stories of people who don't understand what is at stake.

Author Brennan Manning said, "The temptation of the age is to look good without being good."[2] It appears that those who "look good" have a harder time accepting Jesus' offer than those who know who they truly are: weary, anxious, burdened sinners.

When Jesus says that anyone who comes to Him must "hate . . . even their own life" (Luke 14:26), He's asking us to give up our delusions about ourselves and our abilities in light of His all-surpassing power and grace. In the same verse, when He says to "hate [our] father and mother, wife and children," He's asking us to stop pretending we can find what our hearts really need in our human relationships. We can stop basing our identity and worth in anything that cannot ultimately satisfy—whether our work, our busyness, or our relationships. When we come to Him, He will reorder our hearts.

In the law of *small is big*, the seemingly insignificant changes we make in recognizing the truth about ourselves add up to the massive, life-shifting perspective that ensures that our love of and life with Christ become our absolute highest priority.

Take a moment to consider what things in your life are easy to give over to God and which are hard. (I find that it's often the things I think or worry about the most that I'm having the hardest time giving over.) Jot down what comes to mind below:

Easy to give over:	Hard to give over:

⏱ Meditation Moment

Close your time today by imagining yourself following in the footsteps of Jesus as you carry those things on your "hard to give over" list, which are like rocks. Feel the heaviness and weight of the burdens, and then imagine yourself laying down those rocks one at a time, releasing them as you keep in step with Jesus.

Day 5: Hope Makes Change Possible

〰〰〰〰〰〰〰〰〰〰〰〰〰〰〰〰〰〰〰〰〰〰〰〰〰〰〰〰〰〰〰〰

Bible Reading: 1 PETER 1:3-9

As we near the end of this first week, you may wonder whether the laws of miracles really make a difference when it comes to the way you interact with others. You may doubt whether change is really even possible for you—or for the way you experience those around you. Our Creator knows our tendencies to doubt what we cannot see and to give up when the going gets tough. Perhaps this is one reason that resurrection hope is such a central focus of our faith. Let's spend some time defining, understanding, and applying hope to our lives today.

Take a minute to write your definition of hope here:

My guess is that exercise may have been harder than you expected. Often, we have a hard time defining biblical buzzwords like *hope, grace, mercy*. But I've found that when we slow down and really dig into these terms, we discover that they are more relevant than we imagined. Let's look at what the Bible says about hope:

1. Read Hebrews 11:1 and write the definition of our faith as related to hope:

Hope is a relational word—it's related to objects or promises that the "hope-ee" expects to experience.

2. Let's take a short survey of how the Bible connects hope to our faith. Write down what you learn about hope from each passage below:

Romans 5:1-5:

Psalm 31:24:

Psalm 130:5:

Romans 15:4:

2 Corinthians 1:8-10:

As we can see, hope is a robust, active experience of believing that there is more for us in the future than we can see in the present. Hope is about our eternal future—when there will be no more crying or pain, when all that God has planned to be redeemed will be restored, when we will be whole and in complete communion with Christ. But hope is not just about what we see for eternity, but how we live today.

3. Look up Psalm 27:13-14 and copy the passage here:

Hope is about a better tomorrow *right here on earth.* It's about seeing God's goodness manifest through the power of the Holy Spirit *right here in the life you have.* Hope is actively, confidently, trustingly waiting as God transforms your heart and deepens your connection to Him. Because of this hope you are connected to something beyond yourself, able to engage productively with the world, and aware of your part in life's greater story. This is what makes change possible.

 ## Meditation Moment
As you quiet your heart before God, consider the ways you need to experience hope. (Circle all that apply.)

a. I need a more active hope: I often forget that God is at work transforming my heart each day.

b. I need a more confident hope: I tend to doubt that He's interested or engaged in my life.

c. I need a more trusting hope: I've been hurt before and need to experience the love of God in a fresh way.

d. I need a more patient hope: I tend to want to see God work quickly and then give up when my prayers aren't immediately answered.

e. Other:_____

Spend these last minutes in God's presence repeating this week's memory verse. Over the weekend, see if you can fully memorize it.

Memory Moment

I remain confident of this: I will see the goodness of the LORD in the land of the living.

PSALM 27:13

Next week, we'll look at how our beliefs about ourselves determine how well we are positioned for miracle moments. I can't wait to explore with you what God has to say about that!

Father in heaven, we want to love You, we want to trust You, we want to know You. This week we've learned about the ways You see the world quite differently than we do. Give us the faith to believe that Your ways are greater than our ways, and help us grow in our confidence and hope in the way You teach us to love. Amen.

THE HEART OF THE MATTER

∧∧∧∧∧

The best version of you comes from a coordinated dance
of your thoughts and emotions, working in rhythm to help
you understand your needs and accomplish your purposes.
The Miracle Moment, *chapter 4, page 65*

∧∧∧∧∧

This Week's Recommended Reading:
Chapters 3 and 4 in *The Miracle Moment*

THIS WEEK, we continue our exploration of why we shouldn't just hope for miracle moments—we should expect them. The confidence we have in our status as victors and overcomers is directly related to the courage we'll need to acknowledge the connection between our thoughts, emotions, and ability to love others.

Feeling our worth starts with honoring and interpreting our emotions and thoughts, in step with one another.

Tune in to video session 2: "The Heart of the Matter."

Video Notes

Three fundamental beliefs that make up the mindset for miracle moments:

- Our souls are precious to God.
- Because God's nature is love, everything is reordered around that belief.
- If you don't know how to feel your worth, you won't know what's worth fighting for.

Self-awareness is the ability to interpret and connect your thoughts and emotions so you can bring them into alignment with God's will.

Self-awareness is really spirit awareness.

The most difficult person you'll ever manage is you.

 ## A Moment of Reflection

1. In the first section of the video teaching, Nicole compares the soul to a precious metal or rare element. What aspects of the soul's worth are hardest for you to believe?

2. Nicole connects our confidence in our worth with our confidence in engaging with conflict in a healthy way. In what relationships do you feel the most confident even when you disagree? What dynamics are present in those relationships that make that possible?

3. In *The Miracle Moment*, we learn that the brain registers physical sensations (like the ways our body responds to fear, stress, anger, sadness) through our limbic system, the center of our emotions. In other words, before a decision is made, our thoughts literally travel *through* our emotional center. We make decisions through our feelings, although it often happens outside of our awareness. Being connected to our emotions allows us to interpret what they are telling us so we can make more thoughtful decisions. Here's a quick inventory to help you determine whether you have more of a thinking or feeling orientation:

THINKER VS. FEELER IN DECISIONS

Answer the following questions to understand how you view the role of logic and emotion in decision-making. Rate the following responses on a scale of 1 to 5, with 1 being "not like me at all" and 5 being "just like me."

Quiz	Rating
1. When I approach a decision, my first inclination is to make a list of pros and cons.	
2. I can feel tension between two people almost immediately.	
3. A person can think their way into any decision, as long as they are willing to be objective.	
4. I usually feel bad or guilty whenever I have to confront someone or someone disagrees with me.	
5. If it's not logical, it's not valid.	
6. Even when the other party tells me that they aren't emotional about a decision, I often interpret their behavior as negative or dismissive.	

7. When I'm in a conflict, the first thing I do is seek the logical explanation for the issue.	
8. Whether in love or war, thought leads the way and emotions follow.	
9. The tone in which something is said is as important as what's being said.	
10. When someone is hurt or sad, my first reaction is to support them emotionally.	

Scoring[1]	Total
Tally your total from questions 1, 3, 5, 7, and 8. *A score of 20 or more indicates you have a strong Thinking orientation. Similar scores in both boxes indicate a balance between Thinking and Feeling.*	
Tally your total from questions 2, 4, 6, 9, and 10. *A score of 20 or more indicates you have a strong Feeling orientation. Similar scores in both boxes indicate a balance between Thinking and Feeling.*	

So why does all this matter? First, recognizing that good people experience decisions, conflicts, and one another differently is important. Being more logical or more emotional is neither good nor bad. Regardless of our orientation, we all have growing to do—it's just a matter of understanding what that growth will look like because of how we are uniquely made.

In the Word

Learning to honor and interpret our emotions is a critical step toward becoming more aligned in our relationships. But even deeper than that, knowing who we are and what we are worth gives us the confidence to grow more like Christ.

Let's look at what God has to say about the worth of each one of us and then connect that to our growth in self-awareness.

Read the passage below:

It's in Christ that we find out who we are and what we are living for. Long before we first heard of Christ and got our hopes up, he had his eye on us, had designs on us for glorious living, part of the overall purpose he is working out in everything and everyone.

EPHESIANS 1:11-12, MSG

1. What do we "find out" in Christ?

2. What is Christ's overall purpose for us?

3. Let's look at several passages that tell us what we are worth to God. Read the following passages and record what they say about how God regards us and/or what we are living for:

   Psalm 8:

   Matthew 10:29-31:

   Ephesians 2:10:

Romans 8:31-39:

2 Corinthians 3:17–4:1:

Based on what you learned above, write one sentence for yourself that answers these questions: What are you worth, and what are you here for?

Application

Proverbs 4:23 says, "Above all else, guard your heart, for everything you do flows from it." The original word used for "guard" is the same word used for a watchman whose job it is to protect a city or fortress. In other words, God is calling us to be watchmen over our own hearts, vigilantly monitoring what gets in.

Name a belief or thought that you may have let into your heart that is contrary to what God says about you.

Memory Moment

This week's memory moment is from the book of Hebrews:

> Let us draw near to God with a sincere heart and with the full
> assurance that faith brings.
>
> HEBREWS 10:22

I love that this verse covers the deep needs of our heart: It's invitational (let us), it's relational (draw near to God), it's honest (with a sincere heart), and it's secure (our faith brings us full assurance). My challenge is for you to commit this verse to memory, spending a few moments each day repeating it (out loud is best!) until it is hard coded into your memory.

Closing Prayer

Father, You've given us full pardon and assurance through our Savior, Jesus Christ.

Jesus, You've proven with Your life, death, and resurrection that You have overcome death and that You have the right to tell us who we are and what we are worth. You tell us there is no condemnation anymore because You've replaced our sin with Your righteousness.

Holy Spirit, give us the power to believe we are exactly who You tell us we are. Walk with us as we learn to watch over our hearts in a way that aligns us with Your vision for the way we are to love others.

 Daily Rhythms

Have you ever had a time in your life when you won big? Maybe it was an awesome game in high school. Maybe it was a promotion. Maybe it was that time you called in to a radio program and won concert tickets! If you've ever had a brush with victory, you know that exhilarating feeling of unshakable confidence and joy—and maybe even disbelief in your good fortune. I think every little win in life is a mere shadow of the reality of our victory in Christ. And it's from that place of unshakable confidence that our relationships can be transformed. Our belief will inform our perspective—of ourselves and others.

So this week, let's take a look at what it means to be defined by our victory in Christ and allow that truth to shape our awareness of our thoughts, emotions, and reactions.

Day 1: Victors in Christ

Bible Reading: ROMANS 8:31-39

As we turn our attention toward what it means to win in Christ and how we can become more aware of our own reactions so we can live in step with the Spirit, let's turn again to a passage we looked at briefly last week.

1. Make a list of the things that Paul names as potential obstacles that keep us from experiencing the love of Christ (Romans 8:35). Add three of your own.

2. Read Psalm 20:6-7. Who is given victory in this passage? What do they trust in?

3. Now this is where it gets good! Read 2 Corinthians 1:20-22. What three
    things have happened that allow us to stand firm in Christ?

    a.

    b.

    c.

Oh my friends, can you even take that in? The promise from Psalms is for
the anointed. And then 2 Corinthians tells us that *we are the anointed.* When
you have said yes to Jesus as Lord of your life, when you have confessed with
your mouth that Jesus is Lord and believe in your heart that God raised him
from the dead, you *will* be saved (Romans 10:9). Not you "might" be saved. Not
"you'll be saved if you keep getting better." Not "you'll be saved if you can really,
really prove you mean it." Not "you'll be saved if you never sin, never doubt,
and never mess up again." You *will* be saved based only on the confession of
your mouth and the belief of your heart in Christ's saving work. And with that
salvation, you are God's anointed.

The promises of Christ mean that *we are already* standing firm. *We are
already* more than conquerors. *We are already* given the assurance of salvation,
and *we are already* sealed with the Holy Spirit as a guarantee of our standing
with God. That is who we are, not because of our own good deeds but because
of our faith in the promises of Christ. Every promise made in Jesus Christ is
fulfilled in Him—and we have access to that all-conquering power. As we'll
explore, He gives us the ability to stop striving in our relationships and to see
others through His eyes. As Christ moves into our lives, we begin to respond
with greater love and compassion and honesty—even with those who try our
patience or get on our nerves.

Sometimes we need to be reminded of what we have in Christ in order to
bring our hearts before Him in worship and gratitude.

I'd like to invite you to take a few moments to write your own prayer to God, thanking Him for the gift of your salvation. If you aren't sure what to write, turn back to the Romans 8 passage and jot down what no longer separates you from Christ. Don't overthink it; you don't have to pretend with God. Even one or two sentences are enough.

Your Victor's Prayer:

Meditation Moment

For the last few minutes, I invite you to reflect on this week's memory moment, imagining yourself drawing near to God and resting in His inexhaustible love for you.

> Let us draw near to God with a sincere heart and with the full
> assurance that faith brings.
> HEBREWS 10:22

Day 2: Defined in Christ

Bible Reading: JOHN 8:53-59

Before we can align our emotions, words, and actions to engage in confident, loving confrontation, we must learn not to attach our identity to other people's acceptance or approval. Now, this does not mean that we become apathetic or distant from others. But the true pathway to being able to love others freely lies in our ability to not be defined or validated by the limited, fickle nature of human hearts. In *The Miracle Moment*, I explain that I think the person who is most able to enter into loving and healthy conflict is "a self-defined individual with a nonanxious presence" (an idea that originated with Edwin Friedman).[2]

Some Christians balk at the idea of being "self-defined," thinking it means being selfish or self-centered. On the contrary, *self-defined* means that our emotions and thoughts are aligned because we know who we are and what we are worth. That alignment allows us to have healthy boundaries with those who oppose or challenge our values.

Let's look together at a conversation between Jesus and some Jews "who had believed him" (John 8:31). Jesus had told these followers, "If you hold to my teaching, you are really my disciples. Then you will know the truth, and the truth will set you free" (verses 31-32).

To our modern ears, this sounds like a lovely motto, worthy of a bumper sticker or at least a social media post. But for these Jews, the suggestion that they needed to be set free was highly offensive. After all, they already identified themselves as God's chosen people and were fiercely devoted to the idea that their ethnic identity created their freedom. But Jesus turned the idea of ethnic privilege upside down with His all-inclusive promises, not just for the Jew but for all people—alongside His rigorous call to follow Him above all else. So when Jesus started teaching about heart change, not rules—about a lifestyle of radical love, not religion—many disagreed and flat-out argued with him, which is what happens next in the chapter.

Finally, in John 8:53, they said, "Who do you think you are?"

Look at Jesus' interesting initial response in the next verse:

> If I glorify myself, my glory means nothing. My Father, whom you
> claim as your God, is the one who glorifies me. Though you do not
> know him, I know him. If I said I did not, I would be a liar like you, but
> I do know him and obey his word.
> JOHN 8:54-55

1. Underline all the "I" statements that Jesus makes in the passage above.

Jesus is defined exclusively through His relationship with the Father. His proof of that relationship is knowing Him and obeying His word. Christ's obedience and His unshakable trust in their relationship allow Him to stand firm against opposition.

Now **read John 8:58** and write down Jesus' answer to the question "Who do you think you are?":

2. Read Exodus 3:14. What did God call Himself?

In John 8:54-55, we catch a glimpse of the audacious claim of Jesus, who clearly called Himself God. (This would have been considered blasphemy, punishable by death, which is why the Jews tried to stone him!)

If you've believed Jesus is just a good teacher, philosopher, or storyteller who uses parables to bring insight into human behavior, I would encourage you to think again. Life coaches, philosophers, and storytellers are great. But none of those titles contain the power of life and death. No life lessons, no matter how profound, can create a heart of compassion, courage, and other-worldly love for people around you. Not even the greatest teacher in your life has the ability to dwell within you and gift you with the Holy Spirit, who transforms your emotions, thoughts, and desires so you can bear the abundant fruit of love, joy, peace, patience, kindness, goodness, faithfulness, gentleness, and self-control (see Galatians 5:22-23). The only power that can do that kind of work inside of you comes from the one who created you.

So what does it mean to be self-defined? It means having a firm conviction about who we truly are in Christ, an assurance that cannot be shaken by any earthly circumstance.

 ## Meditation Moment

To close this time, turn to Ephesians 4:22-24. This passage gives you a visual picture of what it looks like to live in your new identity. During your five minutes of quiet time with God, listen for what the "old self" might be saying about what you should think about, worry about, or care about. Now imagine putting on your "new self." Visualize the kind of presence, peace, and abundant love you have access to. You might imagine yourself in that "new self" state as you think about a challenging relationship you'll face today. Picture yourself living in the fullness of your identity in Christ, no matter the circumstances.

Day 3: In Step with the Spirit

Bible Reading: GALATIANS 6:1-10

One of the realities of frustrating relationships is that we often experience the worst of ourselves when we interact with those people. When someone misunderstands us, we might feel angry and then guilty about feeling angry over a small slight. When someone is hard to connect with, we may feel fearful and insecure, and then upset with ourselves for not having the courage to speak up. And the person who is hardest to deal with in your life is the one you look at in the mirror every day. You might want to read that again and see if you can take that in: The most difficult person you'll ever manage is you.

This is why remembering the foundational truth of who we are in Christ is so important to our work together. Jesus Christ directly addressed the greatest need of our souls through the Cross, and then He directly addressed the greatest need of our daily lives through the gift of the Holy Spirit. Let's take a look at what we know about the Holy Spirit's work in our lives:

1. Read Galatians 5:16-18. How do you experience the conflict between your sinful nature and the Spirit when it comes to relationships? Choose all that apply:

   a. I often feel anxious and make myself feel better through tasks, achievement, and approval or by comforting myself with food, work, or other behaviors.

   b. I want to love people well, but I have a short fuse and get angry easily.

   c. I've been hurt badly before and don't want to risk letting people in.

   d. The demands on my life feel so pressing. I want to be more engaged in relationships but don't have time.

   e. I don't feel an inner conflict.

2. The passage we just read in Galatians goes on in verses 19-21 to talk about the acts of the sinful nature. I think the fact that these verses include the words "witchcraft" and "orgies" can throw us off, so let's look at some of the *other* words in the passage that apply directly to our relationships. Galatians says that we are living in the power of the sinful nature when we:

    a. Have ongoing discord in our relationships (lack of harmony)

    b. Feel jealous of others

    c. Prioritize our ambition/success over the way we treat people

    d. Experience division or dissension (ongoing arguments/conflict) in our relationships

    e. Act out of anger

    Put an asterisk next to any of these acts of the sinful nature you've experienced in the last week.

What we learn in Galatians is that *when we keep in step with the Spirit (5:25) we will manifest the fruit of the Spirit.* In other words, when we set our hearts and minds on what the Spirit desires, we will naturally experience more Spirit abundance in our relationships.

Friends, I cannot emphasize enough how important it is that we get the order right. You don't just grind out more fruit of the Spirit by trying harder or having more willpower. You don't shame or bully or cheer yourself into producing more fruit of the Spirit. You don't become more fruitful by following a checklist of rules. The fruit of the Spirit is a natural outpouring of a life you are living. You don't get the Spirit in step with your life or your priorities. Rather, you open yourself up to the work of the Spirit in your life so that you can *get in step with the Spirit.*

All of us struggle with the desires of our sinful nature—the way we try to get what we need from others, the way we try to feel good about ourselves. But in the Spirit, we are given the most powerful gift in the universe—resurrection power. It's the power to die to our old ways of living and be raised to a new pattern of love and freedom.

3. Let's take a close look at a prayer in Ephesians:

> I pray that your hearts will be flooded with light so that you can understand the confident hope he has given to those he called—his holy people who are his rich and glorious inheritance.
> EPHESIANS 1:18, NLT

As you answer the questions below, I encourage you to make your responses personal, using I/me/my.

a. What's the goal of this prayer? (phrase following the first "that")
   The goal of this prayer is that my . . .

b. What's the result of this change? (phrase following "so that"—remember, make it personal.)

c. What does God call His holy people? How does He regard you?

4. Now read what the apostle Paul says in another place:

> This same God who takes care of me will supply all your needs from his glorious riches, which have been given to us in Christ Jesus.
> PHILIPPIANS 4:19, NLT

Once again, we see the use of the words *riches* and *glorious*. What does the apostle Paul say happens to you because of God's glorious riches?

Today we've spent some time remembering that miracle moments don't happen because we strive after them. Although all of us can grow in the way we engage and love those around us, for the Christian, this love takes on an entirely different form through Christ. As our hearts become flooded with the light of Christ, our daily lives become awake to keeping in step with the Spirit and God supplies our needs from His own gloriously deep pocket of riches.

Meditation Moment

It can be easy to stop prioritizing these few minutes at the end of each day's session. But Scripture and science agree on this point: Meditation is good for us. David's heart was clearly full of thanksgiving as he wrote Psalm 145:5: "I will meditate on your wonderful works." Recent studies have shown that meditation improves mood, lowers stress, and creates stronger immune function.[3] Our mind, body, and spirit benefit when we spend moments in attentive rest each day.

If you're finding it difficult to build this habit, set your cell phone timer for four minutes, and as we close our time together, I encourage you to enter into the presence of God and recite this truth adapted from Philippians 4:19: *God will provide all my needs today.*

Day 4: The Wise of Heart

Bible Reading: MATTHEW 15:1-18

Today we will spend a few minutes exploring what God means in Scripture when He speaks of the heart and how our engagement with the heart is directly linked to our awareness of the interplay of our thoughts and emotions.

Let's **review Proverbs 4:23**, this time reading it in a few different versions:

Above all else, guard your heart, for everything you do flows from it.
(NIV)

Guard your heart above all else, for it determines the course of your life.
(NLT)

Keep your heart with all vigilance, for from it flow the springs of life.
(ESV)

The word *heart* used in the Old Testament has no English equivalent. It is a word that "combines the complex interplay of intellect, sensibility, and will."[4] The heart is a source of thinking, reflecting, and acting. The heart is at work in our conscious world (where we are aware of our thinking) as well as our subconscious world (where we are prone to reactivity/triggers). The heart is that part of us that communes with and experiences the Spirit of God. The heart can be wise or foolish; it can accept or reject correction, and it can become hardened or calloused in our spiritual life. Above all, "the heart is meant to discern and prompt action."[5]

1. Now that you know its fuller definition, change the word *heart* in the verse into a phrase that more fully captures what it means for you:

   Above all else, guard your _____,
   for everything you do flows from it.

In chapters 4 and 5 of *The Miracle Moment*, we explore the psychology of our emotional life, much of which is generally below our level of awareness. Here's a segment from the beginning of chapter 5:

> Self-awareness is not a goal unto itself. We are not peering inward to the depths of our emotions just to drown in the deep end of everything we've ever felt and experienced. Instead, self-awareness is the first step toward getting more of what we really need in life. Our alignment comes from *meaning what we feel* before *saying what we mean*. To "mean what we feel" is to be able to accurately interpret our emotions—acknowledging the reactions, evaluating whether they are relevant to the situation or relationship in front of us, and then honoring or releasing them.
> *THE MIRACLE MOMENT*, PAGE 75

Let's look at how Jesus made the Pharisees aware of what was driving them.

2. Read Matthew 15:1-18. What happened that made the Pharisees so emotionally triggered? (See verse 2.)

3. Why do you think that Jesus' way of living might have felt threatening to them? (Check out Matthew 23:5-7 for a hint.)

In counseling, we often say that awareness begins by recognizing that "the first problem is not the real problem." In Matthew 15:6-9, Jesus reveals the "real problem" for the Pharisees. What does He determine it is? (See verse 8.)

Likewise, in our own lives, the real problem is usually not the presenting problem. Our first problem might be our lazy coworker, or our unresponsive teenager, or our manipulative brother-in-law. But the real problem is often deeper, hidden—both in us and in the person we are struggling with. Jesus' directive is that where our hearts (our emotions, thoughts, decisions, beliefs) are is where the problem resides.

4. When Jesus calls the crowd to Himself, what does He teach them is the real problem? (See Matthew 15:11.)

5. Now check out Luke 6:44-45. Write down Jesus' words from verse 45:

6. Turn to 1 Peter 1:22 and write the verse here:

When you write out God's truth, you engage with your physical, mental, and spiritual life and allow God to direct you down into the depths of your heart. And it is this willingness to understand the mechanics of your heart—how and why you can react so strongly to other people that you either shut down with silence or blow up with anger and criticism—that enables you to experience the transforming power of God.

In *The Miracle Moment*, I describe how emotional triggers orchestrate so many of our reactions:

> *Emotional triggers* are like the beginning of a well-known song that you can't help but follow the moves to. . . .
> We should especially pay attention when
>
> - our emotional response outweighs a normal reaction to the situation (either good or bad);
> - we find ourselves becoming overly aggressive or overly withdrawn in response to the moment;
> - we feel panic or dread in the moment (often a feeling that centers in the gut and may include sweaty hands or an increased heart rate or breathing); and/or
> - we feel powerless to control our actions ("They made me do it").
> THE MIRACLE MOMENT, PAGES 66, 68

Fortunately, these triggers don't have to have the last word. As we saw in Galatians 5, God promises to transform the fallen nature that often causes us to react in unloving ways without our even thinking. Then we can produce the fruit of the Spirit—but as we've learned this week, it's on us to keep in step with the Spirit, which is the ongoing work of self-awareness.

 ## Meditation Moment

For your last few minutes, turn your mind back to this week's memory verse:

> Let us draw near to God with a sincere heart and with the full assurance that faith brings.
> HEBREWS 10:22

Spend time resting in God's presence as you consider what it would look like for you to live with a "sincere heart" in your thoughts, emotions, and words today.

Day 5: Harnessing the Power

Bible Reading: EPHESIANS 1:17-23

So how do we spot a miracle moment? It looks like your ability to slow down in an interaction, access and interpret your emotions, and commit to the response that reflects who you want to become. When it comes to our self-awareness,

> As long as you hold on to the idea that your reactions are justified, that he/she/they "made" you do it, that you "can't" express your emotions, etc., you have decided that you can't, won't, or don't want to change. . . . And as long as that's the case, you'll have a 100 percent success rate at staying exactly the same.
>
> In order to grow, you have to commit to who you want to be.
>
> *THE MIRACLE MOMENT*, CHAPTER 5, PAGES 83–84

When you commit to keeping in step with the Spirit of God, you are committing to a journey that you aren't in control of! You are committing to be led by God into greater awareness of the patterns that are hindering your ability to love others. You are committing to the courageous work of realigning your emotions, words, and actions for a specific purpose. In Christ, we are not in charge of deciding what we want out of relationships—on the contrary, we are *commanded by God* to engage with people in specific ways. If you've been around church for even ten seconds, you have probably heard this passage shared and preached:

> "Teacher, which is the greatest commandment in the Law?"
>
> Jesus replied: "'Love the Lord your God with all your heart and with all your soul and with all your mind.' This is the first and greatest commandment. And the second is like it: 'Love your neighbor as yourself.' All the Law and the Prophets hang on these two commandments."
>
> MATTHEW 22:36-40

1. There are three "love objects" in these verses. What are they?

   a.

   b.

   c.

2. As we've discussed this week, God didn't just give us a command and then leave us on our own to figure out how to do it. He's given us the gift of the Holy Spirit, the power source behind our transformation. Loving like Jesus is only possible when we have the energy of Jesus in our lives. Let's explore what the Spirit enables us to do as we move from insight to action:

   a. The Holy Spirit gives us the power to know the truth.

      Read John 16:13. What is the Holy Spirit called in this verse?

      What two things will the Spirit do in our life?

   b. The Holy Spirit gives us the power to love.

      Read 2 Timothy 1:7. What does the Spirit give us the power to do?

Flip back to Romans 5:5 and rewrite it as a personal promise from God to you:

c. The Holy Spirit gives us the power to say yes and no.

   I've included a few verses below. Circle the description of what happens when we are responsive to the Spirit and the grace of God:

The Advocate, the Holy Spirit, whom the Father will send in my name, will teach you all things and will remind you of everything I have said to you.
JOHN 14:26

The grace of God has appeared that offers salvation to all people. It teaches us to say "No" to ungodliness and worldly passions, and to live self-controlled, upright and godly lives in this present age.
TITUS 2:11-12

Finally, be strong in the Lord and in his mighty power. . . . Stand firm then, with the belt of truth buckled around your waist, with the breastplate of righteousness in place, and with your feet fitted with the readiness that comes from the gospel of peace. In addition to all this, take up the shield of faith, with which you can extinguish all the flaming arrows of the evil one. Take the helmet of salvation and the sword of the Spirit, which is the word of God.
EPHESIANS 6:10, 14-17

As we ask God to open the eyes of our heart, as we are responsive to the Spirit's guidance and direction in our lives, we experience a power far beyond our own strength. That power is the source of our transformation. It's the power to be curious, not condemning. It's the power to make small changes that lead to new ways of responding and loving those around us.

 ## Meditation Moment

Ask God to "enlighten the eyes of your heart" (see Ephesians 1:18) about the ways you may react to people in response to your own emotional triggers—fear, anger, insecurity, frustration, or selfishness. Even though it's uncomfortable to face your sin, stay close to God with this truth: "He will take great delight in you; in his love he will no longer rebuke you, but will rejoice over you with singing" (Zephaniah 3:17).

When you sit with God in His love, what song or lyrics do you hear Him sing for you?

HUMILITY IN ACTION

∧∧∧∧∧

Expressing yourself . . . is humbling and vulnerable. It requires you to leave the safety of self-righteousness and anger and enter into the wilderness of your own fragility and emotions. It requires you to be open to more hurt, if the other party scorns you or rejects your attempts at reconciliation. But it also creates the space needed for a miracle. It moves you toward a loving, humble stance rather than a judgmental or closed position. It allows for nuance and change and forgiveness. It isn't easy—but it's worth it for the potential of a miracle moment.

The Miracle Moment, *chapter 6, page 103*

∧∧∧∧∧

This Week's Recommended Reading:
Chapters 5 and 6 in *The Miracle Moment*

"PRIDE GOES BEFORE A FALL," a shortened version of Proverbs 16:18, is one of those biblical truths that has permeated popular culture. It's quoted in Broadway plays, bestselling novels, and blockbuster movies. Almost everyone agrees that pride is a problem—but we are far better at seeing it in others than recognizing it in ourselves. This week, we turn our attention to humility and its impact on our relationships. Let's discover together how dying to our own pride sets us free to an entirely different view of love—and enables us to see and seize the miracle moments in front of us.

⭐ How we position ourselves with God, with ourselves, and with others is the critical ingredient for miracle moments.

▶ *Tune in to video session 3: "Humility in Action."*

Video Notes

Humility is always a placement issue.

Our life's work is to learn to "walk in the way of love" (Ephesians 5:2).

Humility is a mindset we can choose.

Three ways to set yourself up for a miracle moment:

1.

2.

3.

 ## A Moment of Reflection

1. Thomas Merton said, "Pride makes us artificial; humility makes us real." Think of the "realest" person you've known in your life. What qualities did they embody?

2. Think of a time when your desire to express why you were right got in the way of reconciliation. If you could have a do-over in that conversation, what would you do differently?

3. How do you define humility? What actions can you observe in a person of humility, particularly in relationships?

In the Word

Andrew Murray, a nineteenth-century South African minister and author, wrote, "There are three great motivations to humility: it becomes us as creatures; it becomes us as sinners; and it becomes us as saints."[1] Let's take a look at how God created us for humility and how that plays out in our relationships.

First, it becomes us as creatures.

Read Revelation 4:9-11. Granted, there is *a lot* going on in this passage. But for our purposes, notice that the elders around the throne are seated in positions of honor and wearing crowns. They are creatures who have been exalted to the highest place.

1. What do the elders do in verse 10?

2. In verse 11, the elders proclaim why God is worthy. What is the reason?

When we consider the fullness of humility, it begins with this vision of creatures in their proper place with their Creator. God Himself models what humility looks like in His triune (three-part) nature. He's not a God who exists in and of Himself. He is a God who exists in perfect communion and community as Father, Son, and Holy Spirit. This may sound quite heady, but remember that we are reordering our understanding of how the world works. One of those discoveries is that God Himself modeled humility and perfect community before He created the world (Genesis 1:26-27; John 1:1-4; 1 Corinthians 8:6)—and will do so again at the culmination of world history, as represented in this passage from Revelation.

We were created to belong in a hierarchy of mutual humility and love.

3. Have you ever felt perfectly small and perfectly safe? Think of a time, perhaps while you were out in nature, when you felt a sense of the greatness of God and the smallness of yourself. Share a few words about how that felt.

Second, it becomes us as sinners.

4. Read 2 Chronicles 7:14. List the actions of people and of God in this passage.

If My people:	Then I will:

5. Why does seeking God's forgiveness require humility?

We were created to experience the deep healing and forgiveness of God as an unearned gift—something we could never do for ourselves.

Third, it becomes us as saints.

The word *saint* might not feel as if it's meant for you, but God uses it to describe us when we've surrendered our lives to Christ. As saints, we are called to a transformed view of ourselves and others.

6. Turn to Romans 12:9-11. Every action listed here connects back to Romans 12:2—they represent the transformation possible only in the Spirit. In which of these actions would you most like to grow?

Transformed by the power of the Spirit, we were created to be humble conduits of God's love to others.

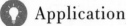

Application

Now that you've explored what Scripture teaches about humility, look back at your definition from "A Moment of Reflection" at the beginning of our lesson. What are you learning about the power of humility in your relationships right now? In what ways do you desire to grow in humility?

Memory Moment

This week's memory moment comes from the apostle John:

> Dear friends, since God loved us that much, we surely ought to love each other. No one has ever seen God. But if we love each other, God lives in us, and his love is brought to full expression in us.
>
> 1 JOHN 4:11-12, NLT

Closing Prayer

Father, it is impossible to fathom how much You love us—but we want to understand it more. Would You give us a curiosity about You and a desire to know Your love more fully? Holy Spirit, move in us, work in us, and lead us to the knowledge of the truth—in our hearts, in our actions, and in our love for those around us. We want Your love to be brought to full expression in us, particularly in those relationships that are challenging today.

In Jesus' name we pray these things, amen.

Daily Rhythms

Last week we explored how the power of the Holy Spirit equips us to be transformed in the way we love. This week, we dive deeper into the outworking of humility in our lives—and how we can begin to season our tough conversations with it.

Day 1: A Miracle Setup

Bible Reading: JOHN 2:23–3:12

To get the most from this week, I encourage you to pay attention to a relationship that may feel hard for you—whether with a relative, a coworker, or a friend. Think of a specific time when you experienced conflict with that person. With that particular incident in mind, engage in your daily devotions with the desire to rewind the game tape of that experience and see what God has to teach you about His love through it.

1. Read John 2:23-24. We looked at the passage about Nicodemus briefly in session 1, but before we look at it again, let's notice what happens right before the conversation between Nicodemus and Jesus. In verse 24, what does it say Jesus would not do?

Here's a longer version of the Greek translation from commentator Dale Bruner:

> Jesus was not trusting himself to them because he knows everyone
> and because he did not need anyone to give him testimony about the
> nature of the human being . . . ; you see, he himself knew quite well
> what is inside the human being.[2]

Friends, this is a key lesson from the person of Jesus that I don't want us to miss. Jesus teaches us that we can love without entrusting our souls to one another. When we know who we are and what we are worth because of our ultimate connection to God, not because of others' validation or approval, we can love with a pure heart. When we are able to connect our worth to God's love, we can love and confront with integrity in our relationships with others.

2. Read John 3:1-12. Notice that in verse 2 Nicodemus uses the word *we*. He is not just a Pharisee—he is a representative, a member of the ruling council. He comes with backup, so to speak. It seems as if Nicodemus is winding up before he gets down to business. But before Nicodemus can steer the conversation, Jesus responds. Record Jesus' first words to Nicodemus in verse 3:

3. Nicodemus responds with two questions. Record them here:

Nicodemus's questions may appear incredulous or skeptical. But let's take a look at another time when Jesus was questioned by religious leaders. In John 9, Jesus heals a man born blind, and a series of events begins to unfold as the Jewish leaders question Jesus' power and His healing on the Sabbath.

4. Read John 9:13-16. What are the two responses of the Pharisees?

5. How would you characterize these answers?

    • Open/curious

    • Questioning

    • Decided

6. Finally, skip ahead to John 9:24. What is the positioning of the Pharisees in this conversation?

• Open/curious

• Questioning

• Decided

In this quick survey of three conversations between Jesus and the Pharisees, notice the progression from openness (Nicodemus) to closed or decided (the Pharisees in 9:24 who "open" their dialogue with a judgment—"We know this man is a sinner").

Even though Nicodemus doesn't immediately proclaim his belief; even though he comes under the cover of night; even though Jesus challenges him—he stays open. He's curious. He continues the dialogue by seeking answers, not making statements of fact. At this point, Nicodemus fades from the narrative . . . until we see him again in John 19:38-42.

7. What is Nicodemus doing in John 19, and what does he bring?

Nicodemus carries a large amount of spices and aloe, usually reserved for royal burials. Nicodemus is a man of few words in the Gospels. He shows up at night and asks two questions. But behind the scenes, something is transforming within him. We may see the miracles of Jesus as the times when He heals the sick or gives sight to the blind or raises the dead. But as Nicodemus illustrates, miracles also happen in the moments when our perspective shifts and we see that perhaps we weren't so right about what we were sure of before. Miracle moments occur when we give up trying to control our relationships by human means, turning instead to the way God designed us to flourish. Our perspective begins to shift when we are willing to be curious and to ask questions rather than give answers.

Now take what you've learned from Nicodemus's curiosity and humility, and consider that tough relationship once more.

8. Rewind a moment of conflict in your life. Think back to how you responded—perhaps with a sharp statement or silent withdrawal. Can you think of a question you could have asked instead? What could you be curious about right now as you remember this conflict?

9. How do you respond when you feel someone doesn't think you are right? Circle the answer that most closely reflects your usual response.

   a. I power up with arguments to prove my point.

   b. I shy away and agree with them to avoid conflict.

   c. I change the topic/deflect with humor but am frustrated on the inside.

   d. I ask questions to try to understand where they are coming from.

   You may find that you react one way in certain situations and differently in others. If you circled more than one answer, in what relationships or circumstances do your responses differ?

A key way to raise your self-awareness is by reshaping your beliefs with humility. For those who answered a or c, humility says, *You are not as right as you think you are.* For those who answered b, humility says, *You are not as wrong as you think you are.*

Humility exists in the openness between right and wrong. It's less about proving ourselves and more about wanting to gain perspective—connecting with another person in a way that creates vulnerability rather than distance.

Meditation Moment

As you close today, reflect on the idea that Jesus "knew quite well what is inside the human being."[3] What are some ways you engage with conflict that you aren't proud of or wish were different? Imagine coming to Jesus with that truth about yourself—even under the cover of night—and listen for His response to you.

Record any thoughts, images, or feelings that come to mind.

Let's close today's study in prayer:

Jesus, You tell us through the story of Nicodemus that life in You isn't about a nice teaching or belief system—it's about being born again. Help me to understand the kind of new birth You want in my relationships, too, and give me the courage to face the truth about myself so that I may receive Your grace.

Day 2: Assume Positive Intent

/\\

Bible Reading: EXODUS 18:8-24

Today we will look at a story that illustrates the good that can come whenever we position ourselves to listen. Let's enter into this story with our hearts attentive to what God wants to teach us.

Read the Exodus passage. A little context: We know that Jethro, Moses' father-in-law, was a leader in his own right in Midian. He was not an Israelite and did not worship the God of Israel.

1. When Jethro visits Moses in the desert, how does he respond to what he learns from his son-in-law (18:8-10)?

2. How much time passes between the time Jethro arrives and when he asks Moses a question in verse 14?

3. Read the passage and take note of Jethro's actions. I'll do the first one for you.

    verse 9: Jethro arrives and praises God

    verse 14: _____

    verse 17: _____

    How does Moses interact with his father-in-law?

    verse 8: Moses tells his father-in-law about everything that has
        happened.

verse 15: _____

verse 24: _____

Moses and Jethro demonstrate mutual respect, even though they are two very different people who do not even believe in the same God. What qualities do you see in both men that make this difficult conversation possible?

4. Notice that Jethro, Moses' elder, humbles himself to listen and observe before he offers Moses help. When you see someone you love doing something you don't think is good, what is your first response?

5. If someone confronts you about something "you are doing [that] is not good," how do the other person's actions affect your willingness to receive the feedback? What actions or attitudes make that more difficult?

6. Read James 3:13 and record it here:

In the story of Moses and Jethro, we see a living example of "deeds done in the humility that comes from wisdom." The first step of engaging with humility in relationships is to start from a posture of openness rather than suspicion. We have a choice to *assume positive intent*—to believe that when we are experiencing conflict or confrontation with another person, there is a good reason for it, one worth discovering.

> Most of us *think* we assume positive intent in others, but the best way to get a baseline on your ability to do so is with a real conflict. Let's try it: Think about a time in the last week when you were irritated, frustrated or hurt by someone. What did you assume about them?
> *THE MIRACLE MOMENT*, PAGES 101–102

Friends, it is easier said than done to assume positive intent. It requires a posture of humility. It requires patience. It requires a willingness to be vulnerable, to choose to let down our guard and receive without trying to force it or fix it before we understand it.

7. For our final reflection of the day, read Philippians 2:5-8:

> In your relationships with one another, have the same mindset as Christ Jesus:
>
>> Who, being in very nature God,
>>> did not consider equality with God something to be used to his
>>>> own advantage;
>> rather, he made himself nothing
>>> by taking the very nature of a servant,
>>> being made in human likeness.
>> And being found in appearance as a man,
>>> he humbled himself
>>> by becoming obedient to death—
>>>> even death on a cross!

Underline the word *mindset*. How would you summarize the mindset God calls us to have in our relationships with one another? What else does this passage say about the way we are to engage with other people?

Meditation Moment

In your final five minutes of today's study, draw near to God in silence. Allow the Spirit of God to bring to mind any relationships in which you have not been assuming positive intent. Ask God to give you a renewed mind and attitude that reflect the mindset of Jesus, perhaps reading through 1 John 4:11-12 again as you do:

> Dear friends, since God loved us that much, we surely ought to love each other. No one has ever seen God. But if we love each other, God lives in us, and his love is brought to full expression in us.
>
> 1 JOHN 4:11-12, NLT

Day 3: Seek to Understand

Bible Reading: COLOSSIANS 3:12-17

The only way to consistently put others before yourself and be able to discern the goodness and humanity in every person is to live into the mindset of Christ.

Now, at this point you might be wondering, *But what if I've been wronged? What if I'm the one being misunderstood?* If that's where you are—hold tight, we will soon get to that! Putting on the mindset of Christ is *not* about becoming a doormat or never being honest about your own hurt or struggle. In reality, it's when we learn humility that we are equipped to enter into our own desires and needs with freedom. This is the miracle of life in Christ. When we release our need, we receive. And as we receive, we can enter into healthy conflict with courage.

1. Read through the Colossians passage twice. Write down at least five instructions that stick out to you in this passage:

    •

    •

    •

    •

    •

Now, think about a relationship in your life where you desire more closeness. It could be with a spouse, child, parent, or friend; it does not need to be someone with whom you have conflict. In many ways, improving our engagement is sometimes easier in relationships that are already strong. With the Colossians instructions in mind, think of a way you could serve that person this week.

Commit to an action here:

2. *Practicing positive intent* and *seeking to understand* are skills that work when relationships are good—and when they are hard. A posture of humility makes good relationships even better, but it can also create miracle moments in tough relationships. Think about a difficult interaction you had recently. What would practicing positive intent and seeking to understand have looked like in that situation? How might these actions have affected the outcome?

 ## Meditation Moment

Turn your heart back to our memory Scripture for the week:

> Dear friends, since God loved us that much, we surely ought to love each other. No one has ever seen God. But if we love each other, God lives in us, and his love is brought to full expression in us.
>
> 1 JOHN 4:11-12, NLT

Take the middle section of verse 11 ("we surely ought to love each other") and meditate on these words in your heart for five minutes:

> *Lord,*
> *Help me to be quick to listen,*
> *slow to speak, and*
> *slow to get angry.*
> *Let your love be my love today.*

Day 4: Own All You Can

Bible Reading: MATTHEW 5:21-24

The standard that God calls us to through Christ is an active, self-sacrificing, intentionally humble love that doesn't just respond to hurt but actively works to repair it. This type of love isn't produced within us naturally; it is a miracle that results from the Holy Spirit's work within us. Let's draw near to Jesus as He leads us into this miraculous kind of love for one another.

1. Read Matthew 5:21-24. In verse 23, what two things does Jesus connect to each other?

"Offering your gift at the altar" is an example of worship, which is the central part of our faith. In other words, in this verse Jesus intertwines our experience of coming into God's presence with our experience of human relationships.

2. What does Jesus say to do first before coming with our gift to God (verse 24)?

3. Who is responsible for the reconciliation?

Once again, we are confronted by what feels like the impossible nature of God's ethic for our lives. But this is the central aspect of our faith. God calls us to what feels like impossible love for others. Our inability to do so humbles us to seek Him again, and in seeking Him we are equipped for miracle moments. It is not a linear progression upward, but a cycle of repentance and growth with God and with others.

4. How do you feel when you think about God's call for us to discern when someone has something against us and then reconcile quickly?

    a. I can think of people in my life whom I don't want to reconcile with.

    b. I like the idea, but I'm not sure how to do it.

    c. Sometimes I'm OK with it; sometimes I'd rather just ignore it.

    d. It depends on whether I feel they're justified in what they have against me.

    e. Honestly, I don't feel like people have any problems with me.

How you respond here is between you and God, so don't worry about what other people might say about your response. If you can't be honest with God, you won't be honest with yourself and you certainly won't be open to miracle moments. In fact, one of the ways to become more connected to God is to begin to engage honestly with the way you conduct yourself in relationships. When you are aware of the ways you do (and don't) love other people, you are more aligned and in touch with the deeper places in your heart that may be responding to others out of distrust, fear, pride, or insecurity.

One of the best ways to test your humility is to commit to true apologies. Here's a definition from *The Miracle Moment*:

> It is easy to offer a conditional apology, which follows the format of "I'm sorry, but . . ." followed by a long and detailed defense of our actions. It is harder to give a true apology with no conditions, which follows this pattern:
>
> > I was wrong.
> > I'm sorry.
> > I would like to make it right.
> > I will do better next time.
>
> *THE MIRACLE MOMENT*, PAGE 110

 ## Meditation Moment

A powerful way to grow in our humility with others is to grow in humility with God first. Think of some ways you've sinned against God this week. If you can't name any specific sins, read through any part of the Sermon on the Mount (Matthew 5–7) to understand what God is calling us to as followers of Jesus. Bring to God your failings, shortcomings, and intentional actions that have gone against His commands. As you do, keep in mind this truth from Psalm 119:132: "Turn to me and have mercy on me, as you always do to those who love your name."

My friend, God's response to your confession is always the same—it's an unconditional offer of His presence, His closeness, and His forgiveness for you. Remember that when you come to Him in confession, God meets you with His mercy every single time. If you need help believing that, you may want to try using this pattern as you bring each specific truth to God:

> *God, I have sinned against You this week by* _____.
> *I receive Your love, mercy, and forgiveness.*

The more aware you are of God's reconciling love and forgiveness for you, the easier it is to seek reconciliation with and forgiveness from others, no matter the circumstances.

Day 5: The Freedom of Humility

Bible Reading: 1 JOHN 4:7-21

Assuming positive intent, seeking to understand, and owning all we can (being good apologizers) in our relationships may sound like a great plan. However, God isn't calling us to a great human plan; He's calling us to a divine disruption of our understanding of humility and love. God doesn't want us to become people who take the right actions with others—He wants us to become righteous people. Rather than "doing the right thing" out of the strength of our will, God changes our will, which makes us desire to do the right thing. Rather than loving people out of our own strength (impossible when it comes to difficult people), God is calling us to be so strong in His love that *we can't help* but love even the most difficult people in our life.

Read the passage below. Underline the words *love, loves,* or *loved.*

> Dear friends, let us continue to love one another, for love comes from God. Anyone who loves is a child of God and knows God. But anyone who does not love does not know God, for God is love.
>
> God showed how much he loved us by sending his one and only Son into the world so that we might have eternal life through him. This is real love—not that we loved God, but that he loved us and sent his Son as a sacrifice to take away our sins.
>
> Dear friends, since God loved us that much, we surely ought to love each other. No one has ever seen God. But if we love each other, God lives in us, and his love is brought to full expression in us.
>
> 1 JOHN 4:7-12, NLT

1. How many times does the word *love, loves,* or *loved* show up in the passage?

2. That's a lot of love! How did God show us how much He loves us?

3. Verse 11 says, "Dear friends, since God loved us that much, we surely ought to love each other." The word *since* connects two thoughts. What two thoughts are hinged on each other?

4. Underline the last sentence in the passage. Do not miss the significance here—what a powerful statement. Based on what you've learned this week, how do you think loving one another brings God's love "to full expression in us"?

5. Now turn to this passage in your Bible and read verses 18-19. We will explore this topic more fully next week, but what fears sometimes keep you from offering the kind of sacrificial love we've discussed this week?

Meditation Moment

During your five minutes of silence, I invite you first to meditate on the loving nature of God, because "perfect love drives out fear" and the only source of perfect love is God. We know that "God is love," which means that every pure expression of love we've experienced in this world is a tiny fragment or a momentary preview of the fullness of God's love for us. Reflect on a moment in your life when you felt loved by someone, and then allow God to show you how His love for you is so much greater than even your greatest moment of love on earth. *The more we understand His love for us, the more we will live out that love in our relationships.*

In your final few minutes of silence, reflect once more on this week's memory passage.

> Dear friends, since God loved us that much, we surely ought to love each other. No one has ever seen God. But if we love each other, God lives in us, and his love is brought to full expression in us.
>
> 1 JOHN 4:11-12, NLT

NO FEAR IN LOVE

∧∧∧∧∧

*When we live in fear, we allow our influence, our contribution,
and our legacy to be stolen from those who need it. As long
as we let fear manage a relationship, a job, or our leadership,
we will be less than who we were intended to be.*
The Miracle Moment, *chapter 7, pages 119–120*

∧∧∧∧∧

This Week's Recommended Reading:
Chapter 7 of *The Miracle Moment*

FIRST JOHN 4:18 SAYS, "The one who fears is not made perfect in love." The original Greek word for "made perfect" is more precisely translated as "completed" or "finished by." I like to think of it as the process of becoming progressively more whole in Christ; it's an ongoing journey of growth that we are on every day of our lives. This week, let's engage in the process of being "made perfect" by learning to better understand our fear and the fear triggers of others, and learning new ways to be both courageous *and* vulnerable. As we do, we can pursue healthy communication with clarity and love.

Conflict threatens our deepest instincts that seek security and validation. Connection creates the safety needed for compromise and reconciliation.

Tune in to video session 4: "No Fear in Love."

Video Notes

Conflict triggers subconscious fears that show up as defensive reactions.

Weapons may form but they will not prosper (Isaiah 54:17).

_____, _____, and _____ create the connection required for nondefensive conflict.

 ## A Moment of Reflection

All of us have conflict styles—specific reactions to conflict. Consider your likely responses to the following examples:

1. You discover that a coworker has been grumbling about how you dropped the ball on a project you worked on together. You know that it was actually your boss who told you to pause on the project and work on her more urgent need first. What is your immediate reaction when you hear about your coworker's complaints?

   a. You feel righteous anger. You can immediately think of five different ways this coworker has let *you* down, and you want to complain about them to someone else.

   b. You feel upset and ashamed. You hate that your coworker would think so poorly of you and tell someone else about it. You commit to double down on your work and get both projects done, but you don't plan to confront your coworker about what you've heard.

c. You are mad. You imagine barging into your coworker's office to tell that person what you think about how they are running their mouth.

d. You feel neutral. You know that people talk about people all the time. It's not your job to make your coworker happy; it's your job to do the work. You ignore what you've heard and decide to let the situation resolve itself.

2. You have felt distant from your spouse lately, but you aren't sure why. When you tried to engage in conversation last evening, your spouse seemed more interested in the TV than in you. You made another attempt today by bringing up an issue with one of the kids that concerns you. Your spouse offers a quick solution that feels hasty and harsh. What is your immediate reaction?

a. You feel righteous anger. You can immediately think of all the ways you support your spouse; you call a friend to vent.

b. You feel hurt. It's hard enough to try to be vulnerable, but now that you've been rebuffed twice, you figure your spouse just isn't interested in connecting.

c. You are mad. You want to respond with insults or criticism.

d. You are neutral. Maybe your issues aren't such a big deal; they will probably get better soon.

These scenarios were designed to get you in touch with your natural instinct in conflict (which we all have)—no one naturally responds to conflict without an emotional response. Your response may be to vent (a); to self-blame (b); to snap back (c); or to shut down (d).

Self-control is about honoring your emotions, but then carefully choosing how to respond to the other person. Think about a time recently when a conflict was resolved in a healthy way (it could have been a small conflict!). How did you work through your instinctual reaction to get to a healthier place?

In the Word

Let's look a little closer at the relationship between Mary, Martha, and Jesus. **Read Luke 10:38-42.**

1. What is Martha's conflict? What is her reaction to conflict in this passage?

2. How does Jesus address her request?

3. Now turn to John 11:4-7, 17-44. It's a longer passage, so you may want to take turns reading it aloud if you are in a group. Listen for Mary's and Martha's reactions to their pain and confusion at Jesus' late arrival.

4. How does each sister react in pain?

5. What does Jesus call the higher purpose of Lazarus's death? (See verses 4 and 40.)

Application

1. Have you ever considered how conflict could be used for God's glory in your life? In what ways does conflict invite you to grow:

   a. in your faith?

   b. in your character?

   c. in your relationships?

2. In your life specifically, where do you want to grow in your reaction and response to conflict?

Memory Moment

Our memory verse this week takes us deeper into 1 John 4, where we are given a beautiful picture of the power of love over fear:

> There is no fear in love. But perfect love drives out fear, because fear has to do with punishment. The one who fears is not made perfect in love.
>
> We love because he first loved us.
>
> 1 JOHN 4:18-19

Closing Prayer

Lord, as we seek to strengthen our relationships, help us look to You first for the compassion, validation, and commitment we crave. Thank You for Your unending and unconditional compassion and love. May it move us to care for and validate others in a way that points them back to You. In Jesus' name, amen.

 Daily Rhythms

This week, we are continuing our growth in self-awareness as we tackle our reactions—the often-unrecognized fears that drive us—and the fears that drive the people we want to understand! As we grow in our discernment of these fear triggers, we will also be able to begin to help defuse reactions through our courageous vulnerability and love. Let's get started!

Day 1: Overcoming Reflexive Reactions

〰〰〰〰〰〰〰〰〰〰〰〰〰〰〰〰〰〰〰〰〰〰〰〰〰〰〰〰〰〰〰〰〰〰〰〰〰〰〰

Bible Reading: ROMANS 12:14-21

In order to transform conflict into connection, we have to be in touch with our own fear triggers, as well as grow in discernment about fear triggers in others. Although we cannot own responsibility for other people's reaction to us (Galatians 6:5), we are called to do everything we can to "do good to everyone" (Galatians 6:10, ESV). Part of the reason we've spent so long on gaining self-awareness is so that we can understand our own reactions, which can create deeper compassion for the reactions of others.

Look at Romans 12:20-21 in the following three translations:

New International Version
On the contrary: "If your enemy is hungry, feed him; if he is thirsty, give him something to drink. In doing this, you will heap burning coals on his head." Do not be overcome by evil, but overcome evil with good.

New Living Translation
Instead, "If your enemies are hungry, feed them. If they are thirsty, give them something to drink. In doing this, you will heap burning coals of shame on their heads." Don't let evil conquer you, but conquer evil by doing good.

The Message
Our Scriptures tell us that if you see your enemy hungry, go buy that person lunch, or if he's thirsty, get him a drink. Your generosity will surprise him with goodness. Don't let evil get the best of you; get the best of evil by doing good.

1. Record the three different phrases used to describe winning over evil:

   a.

   b.

   c.

2. In *The Miracle Moment*, we learn about five different fears that are triggered by conflict: fear of being violated (hurt), fear of loss of control, fear of rejection, fear of failure, and fear of loss/death (losing a relationship permanently).[1] What fear triggers are you most likely to react to?

Let's look at two places in Scripture that give us a sense of how evil is overcome. You may not think the word *evil* applies to this situation, so let's rephrase it as "anything that comes between you and God's way for holy living." With that in mind:

3. Turn to Proverbs 8:13. What four things does God hate?

4. Turn to Proverbs 16:6. What has the power to turn away evil?

5. Read Psalm 23 slowly a few times, paying attention to the ways God desires to remove our fears. According to Psalm 23:4, what keeps us from fearing evil?

A shepherd used the rod and staff to fend off enemies and keep the sheep from going astray. He would rescue or disentangle sheep caught in bushes or brambles. The rod and staff symbolize guidance, safety, and protection.

 ## Meditation Moment

As you draw near to God, imagine carrying your fears into His presence. Think of the ways you try to protect yourself in conflict: with anger, control, or withdrawal. Imagine laying those down and simply allowing Him to guide and protect you.

Day 2: Understanding Fear, Part 1

Bible Reading: JOHN 18:28–19:16

Over the next two lessons, we will look at one story of conflict that illustrates the difference between a life of fear and a life of love. The story is of the interaction between Pilate, the appointed governor over Judea,[2] and Jesus during His arrest, trial, and ultimate crucifixion. The story is long, but the power is in the details, so let's slow down and jump into this fascinating account.

1. Write down Pilate's initial questions of Jesus when he brings Him into his headquarters for a private conversation (verses 33-38):

   a.

   b.

   c.

   d.

2. What does Jesus tell Pilate His ultimate purpose is?

3. Although Pilate says he finds "no guilt in him" (verse 38, ESV), the governor still makes a concession at the beginning of chapter 19. What does Pilate do to avoid additional confrontation?

4. John 19:8 gives us a window into Pilate's motivation. What does it say about Pilate's state of mind and heart?

5. The Gospel of Matthew provides additional insight into this moment. Turn to Matthew 27:15-23. What message did Pilate receive from his wife that may have caused him additional tension?

6. What did Pilate recognize was the motivation behind the Jewish leaders' insistence on Jesus' crucifixion (Matthew 27:18)?

7. Notice Pilate's reaction to the conflict between his own conscience and the insistence of the crowd regarding his decision. What are two to three things you've learned about your own reaction to conflict?

Meditation Moment

Spend a few minutes thinking about the different ways you act when you are experiencing love versus how you act when experiencing fear (or anything that doesn't feel like love). What does an environment of love do for you?

Let's close by taking our memory Scripture for the week and rewriting it as a prayer. I've started it for you:

> There is no fear in love. But perfect love drives out fear, because fear has to do with punishment. The one who fears is not made perfect in love.
>
> We love because he first loved us.
>
> 1 JOHN 4:18-19

Personal Prayer:

Father, You tell me that there is no fear in love and that Your perfect love drives out fear. But I confess I still feel fear about _____. Lord, I want to allow my fears in conflict to teach me about deeper places of love and trust with You. I specifically bring _____ [person or circumstance] to you right now and ask You to give me love and courage to _____.

Day 3: Understanding Fear, Part 2

Bible Reading: JOHN 18:28-19:16

Today let's journey back into the interaction between Jesus and Pilate and look at how the actions of Jesus point us to a higher love. Take your time reading and absorbing Jesus' words. If it feels deep or even confusing, that's OK! Remember that *chaos before order* means we might need to be uncomfortable or even disturbed before we move toward a new way of living.

1. What question does Jesus ask Pilate in John 18:34?

Jesus gives Pilate an entry point to curiosity. He seems to be asking, "Do you really want to know?" So often when we are in conflict with others, we need to start by asking ourselves honestly, *Do I really want to know?*

Jesus responds to Pilate about the way of His Kingdom. Let's recall Jesus' ultimate purpose statement and invitation, which Pilate didn't realize was the single most important moment of his life (verse 37).

2. Now flip back to the story of Nicodemus. What was Jesus' last statement to Nicodemus (John 3:21)?

3. When Jesus encountered the woman at the well, what did He say His Father seeks most from people (John 4:23)?

We ultimately have to decide if we believe in and want truth in our lives. Truth has to become more important to us than fear. We must be open to the truth of our own hearts, the truth of the way we intentionally or unintentionally hurt others, and the truth of what it takes to forgive, reconcile, and trust. As long as the power of our fear is stronger and more active than our belief in truth, we will, like Pilate, ultimately live from a position of questioning—"What is truth?" (verse 38). We will be "like a wave of the sea, blown and tossed by the wind" (James 1:6). There is only one reason we can move toward difficult truth. There is only one reason we can choose love over fear.

4. Turn to John 1:14. What does it say Jesus is "full of"?

_____ and _____

Meditation Moment

Author Henri Nouwen says, "At issue here is the question: 'To whom do I belong? God or to the world? . . . The world's love is and always will be conditional. As long as I keep looking for my true self in the world of conditional love, I will remain 'hooked' to the world—trying, failing, and trying again. It is a world that fosters addictions because what it offers cannot satisfy the deepest craving of my heart."[3]

Christ is ultimate truth and total grace. It is only because of His unconditional acceptance that we can have the courage to see who we really are—and be transformed into people of ever-increasing grace and truth. It is grace that gives us courage to face and confront the truth in ourselves and others. It is grace that says, "I am not finished growing, and neither are you. We can love each other in our need for grace in this moment."

For the rest of this week, devote your meditation space to bringing a relationship before God that you desire to see grow, deepen, or heal. As you think about that person, what feelings come up?

Spend a few minutes thinking about this person and the idea of Jesus being full of grace and truth. Picture Him guiding and leading this relationship. There is no need to resolve any feelings now—just allow space to hold these things in the presence of the Spirit.

Day 4: The Power of Validation

Bible Reading: JAMES 3:13-18

So far this week, we've done a deep dive into the power that fear, envy, and ambition have to keep us from the truth. We've also examined the courage needed to face the truth for ourselves and for others. Now we are going to move into a practical examination of how we can care for others during conflict in a way that moves us toward connection rather than division.

Consider these words from the book:

Defusing fear involves solidifying an environment of safety by conveying the inherent worth of each person's presence. It's about leaders first acknowledging their commitment to the people around them to defuse any fear of rejection. Next, great leaders remind themselves and their team of the common purpose to help them recognize the value of working through the conflict. Conveying commitment to the purpose draws everyone in the conflict toward one another with shared goals, rather than away from each other in an attempt to defend their own egos.

THE MIRACLE MOMENT, CHAPTER 7, PAGE 126

1. In James 3:13-18, what does the author identify as the fruit of a wise and understanding life?

2. List the qualities of wisdom from heaven found in verses 17-18.

One of the most powerful qualities of a peacemaker is the ability to use words to convey compassion, empathy, and belonging. This kind of validation creates safety to confront more difficult truths.

3. Yesterday we learned that Jesus is "full of grace and truth" (John 1:14). When it comes to conflict, we all exist in what might feel like the tension between grace and truth. Plot yourself on the following scale:

MY CONFLICT STYLE

I arc toward grace. God is a God of mercy and calls us to forgive and trust one another, and I'd rather not confront.

I arc toward truth. God is a God of justice and calls us to seek and confront the truth with one another, and I admit I don't forgive easily.

Grace   Truth

It often feels like these two characteristics cannot coexist. Yet they do exist perfectly in the person of Jesus. If you arc toward the grace side, you may find yourself overemphasizing the nature of Jesus to forgive—and yes, He represents 100 percent forgiveness—but He does not shy away from conflict. And if you arc toward the truth side, you may find yourself overemphasizing truth—and yes, Jesus is "the truth"—but the way He invites people into that truth is with His gentle and humble heart. Here is a more realistic version of the diagram:

Distance/disorder   Grace/truth

When we feel threatened or defensive because of a confrontation, frustration, or hurt, we react from our own self-protective stance before considering the other person. But miracle moments come when we shift from a position of protecting ourselves to validating the other party. Validation is the way we convey our commitment to both truth and grace in our relationships.

4. Now skim through Proverbs 15, looking for instruction on the words of the wise. Jot down two or three reflections on what wisdom looks like when it comes to our speech.

 Meditation Moment

From *The Miracle Moment*, page 128:

> Conveying commitment for safety sounds like this:
>
> - I believe in you (trust).
> - I want to be on your team (vision).
> - I like you (acceptance).
> - I would like to know what you think (value).
>
> Conveying commitment helps create an environment of safety. It says to people, "You are safe to bring your vulnerable fears into my presence." It allows people to freely express themselves because you are addressing the fears that keep people from being free. When your words and actions tell the people you love or lead that they are trusted, they belong, and they are valued, people feel safe to be human: needs, fears, flaws, and all.

What would conveying commitment look like in your most important relationships today? These could be words of approval and encouragement that you deliver in person, via text, or on the phone. As you draw near to God in these final minutes, ask Him to bring to your mind a person whom you could validate today with your words. (Then go and do it!)

Day 5: Putting It into Practice

Bible Reading: JAMES 3:17-18; 1 PETER 3:14-16

You finished day 4 by praying for someone and then thinking about how you might validate them. Did you follow through? If not, consider sending a text right now or making a note in your calendar to do so later today. Aligning our lives for miracle moments means putting our words into practice. The more consistent you are in pursuing small changes, the greater the transformation over time!

In a Bible study, it can be easy to plow through material without checking in with ourselves to see how well we are retaining and being transformed by the information we are consuming. Perhaps it's due to the insecurity of your Bible teachers (including me!), who feel as if giving you so much knowledge will somehow assure your growth. But when we step back and think about it, insight often comes like a sunrise—slow, subtle, and gentle. Rather than more information, today I want to invite you to take these fifteen minutes to reflect on what you are learning, and to pause and celebrate how far you've already come.

Let's use our memory Scriptures as a guide. I encourage you to flip back through this guide, reviewing your notes or Scriptures, or revisiting any places where you got stuck or sidetracked. I've given you some questions to consider, but if you prefer, you can do a self-guided reflection and use the space at the end of this lesson to record your own impressions or prayers, particularly to express gratitude to God for how He's meeting you and where you are growing.

Memory Moment #1

I remain confident of this: I will see the goodness of the LORD in the land of the living.
PSALM 27:13

1. In session 1, we reviewed the five laws of miracles. Turn back to page 8. What law do you see at work in your life? Which one is most difficult to put into practice?

Memory Moment #2

Let us draw near to God with a sincere heart and with the full assurance that faith brings.

HEBREWS 10:22

2. In session 2, we looked at our identity in Christ as overcomers, and what it looks like to be in step with the Spirit in our self-awareness and in relationships. Over these past weeks, where have you been growing in self-awareness?

Memory Moment #3

Dear friends, since God loved us that much, we surely ought to love each other. No one has ever seen God. But if we love each other, God lives in us, and his love is brought to full expression in us.

1 JOHN 4:11-12, NLT

3. In session 3, we turned our attention to how conflict invites us to deeper places of humility. What does it look like for you to grow in humility with God and with others?

Memory Moment #4

There is no fear in love. But perfect love drives out fear, because fear has to do with punishment. The one who fears is not made perfect in love.

   We love because he first loved us.

1 JOHN 4:18-19

4. This week, we looked at fear signals in ourselves and in others, and we explored our own relationship with grace and truth. What fears are most triggered in you by conflict?

Meditation Moment

Use the space here to celebrate the insights you've gained and places you've grown since beginning this study. Remember, *chaos before order* and *small is big*.

SEEK RESTORATION

When trust has been breached, it doesn't come back naturally. Working toward change and rebuilding trust are not for the timid. It takes time, communication, and commitment. It takes a willingness to try and fail, and try again. But this step is the fortifying agent of your soul. It's where real change happens. Not every relationship makes it to this stage, but for those that do, it is the binding agent of humanity, bringing out the strength and resilience within.

The Miracle Moment, *chapter 8, page 141*

This Week's Recommended Reading:
Chapters 8 and 9 in *The Miracle Moment*

WE ALL GET HURT IN RELATIONSHIPS. When we love, we open ourselves up to that possibility. But most of us have never learned how to go beyond "I'm sorry" in the way we relate and rebuild after hurt. Restoring trust takes more than an apology. In this week's lesson, we'll learn what reconciliation is, how and when it's possible, and how to rebuild after trust has been breached.

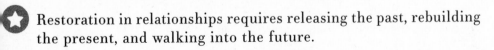 Restoration in relationships requires releasing the past, rebuilding the present, and walking into the future.

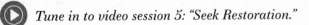 *Tune in to video session 5: "Seek Restoration."*

Video Notes

Love is an active choice to move toward the common good (1 Corinthians 13:6).

Three stages of growing in love and connection in relationships:

1.

2.

3.

Trust is built and rebuilt not only with words but with actions.

Three parts of a real apology:

1.

2.

3.

Forgiveness and reconciliation aren't the same thing.

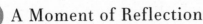

A Moment of Reflection

Take a moment to complete a self-score inventory that will give insight into your practices around the process of reconciliation:

1. Using the scale below, evaluate your tendency when it comes to asking for forgiveness from 1 (I really try to not need forgiveness) to 5 (I frequently ask for forgiveness from family and friends):

```
|_____|_____|_____|_____|
1                2                3                4                5
```

2. Using the scale below, evaluate your tendency when it comes to receiving forgiveness and moving forward from 1 (I find it hard to let go when I've been wronged) to 5 (I forgive easily):

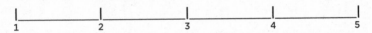

```
|_____|_____|_____|_____|
1                2                3                4                5
```

3. What's your instinctive response when someone breaks your trust?

   a. I want to confront the issue and try to rebuild the relationship. How we rebuild is an important sign of how close the relationship can be.

   b. I want to forgive and forget—but I hope they don't do it again.

   c. I want to distance myself; once I've lost trust, it's almost impossible to get it back.

For many people in the church, our understanding and definition of love, forgiveness, and trust have gotten all mixed together in the word *nice*. Somehow we've received the message that having and holding to our boundaries and taking time to build trust in relationships are not "nice" to do. And that's why we started with the miracle moment law that *nice is bad*. The love God calls us to with one another is much stronger than nice. It's a love that can forgive even the worst transgression—but it also calls you to "guard your heart" (Proverbs 4:23) and be "shrewd" in your relationship with others (Matthew 10:16). To be shrewd means to be aware that you are prone to sin—and so is the other party. To be shrewd means to recognize that reconciliation is a process, not a transaction, and that rebuilding trust takes time and intentionality.

In the Word

When you look back at your reflection questions, do you have a sense of what the "right" answers are? If you answered that you forgive and receive forgiveness easily and that you confront and rebuild in your relationships, then you are living in a healthy space. For most of us, though, one issue—or all three—around forgiving others, accepting forgiveness, and reconciling well is not easy to come by. But remember—*curiosity not condemnation*. There is a reason for the things you do; even more so, there is a rationale behind your pattern of behavior. Be gentle with yourself as you grow. New practices take time and effort to develop.

Let's turn to John 21 for a picture of what healthy reconciliation looks like:

1. Read John 21:15-25 aloud if you are in a group. As you listen to the story, pay attention to how you imagine the emotion between Jesus and Peter as this conversation unfolds. For context, be aware that this is immediately after Jesus' resurrection.

This passage is a picture of what reconciliation requires . . . releasing the past, rebuilding the present, and walking into the future.

What do you notice about Peter's engagement with Jesus? Write down three to five observations from the passage.

Let's rewind the game tape and see what happened before this moment.

2. Turn to Luke 22:31-32. What does Jesus predict will happen? What does He ask Peter to do after trust is rebuilt?

3. Read Matthew 26:34-35, 69-75. What is Peter's response to his own failure?

Friends, even if this story is familiar to you, I invite you to return to it with the full heart and mind it requires. Peter's heart-wrenching conversation with Jesus must have left him feeling exposed and vulnerable. Imagine being in Peter's position, receiving these words with full knowledge of his own failure. No excuses, no justification, no shifting of blame. Just Jesus, knowing full well what Peter has done, and desiring to receive him back. Now in order to fully engage with the story, we have to use our imagination.

4. Going back to John 21, we read in verse 17 that "Peter was hurt." When you imagine yourself in Peter's place, why would this conversation leave you feeling hurt?

When we breach trust in relationships, it is painful. But genuine healing from the rift can also be painful. It requires us to enter into our own failing without excuses. It requires us to receive forgiveness we don't deserve. It requires us to offer forgiveness we might not want to give. It requires us to change the way we relate moving forward. It opens us up to more hurt, because we are coming back to the offender, but it is also the only way to a stronger bond and a deeper connection.

5. How does your understanding of grace and forgiveness in Christ change the way you want to engage with reconciliation in your relationships? Is there a relationship in your life that you want to deepen or repair?

6. Finally, let's write out two important verses that will inform our learning this week:

Romans 14:19

Ephesians 4:3

What do both verses call us to do in relationship with one another?

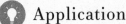

Application

Where do you need to exert more effort in your relationships? Circle all that apply, or write in your own answer:

a. I want to be more aware of how my own reactions are impacting others.

b. I want to know how to be more vulnerable with my responses.

c. I need to know how to stand up to what's wrong and become stronger in my convictions.

d. I don't know how to move forward after I've been hurt.

e. I want to stop talking about people behind their backs and instead resolve problems with them directly.

f. I need to remember that my perception of the relationship is not the only possible interpretation.

g. _____

I encourage you now to bring your requests before God. Scripture tells you and me that we don't have to be anxious about making our requests, but with thanksgiving, we can bring them before God (Philippians 4:6). No request is too big or too small, no fear too trivial or too overwhelming. If you are in a group, I encourage you to spend the remainder of this time together to share where you want to "make every effort" and then pray for one another. Remember, it is God who transforms our hearts (Romans 12:1-2). Our job is to keep in step with the Spirit as He does His renovation work.

Memory Moment

Let us therefore make every effort to do what leads to peace and to mutual edification.

ROMANS 14:19

Closing Prayer

Father in heaven, You've promised in Your Word that I can bring every request before You. As I think about where You are calling me deeper in my relationships, I specifically bring the following situation before You: _____. Thank You, Father, that You are the one who transforms my heart. I ask that anywhere I am reacting, resenting, or withdrawing, You would heal my heart, strengthen my faith, and give me the courage and confidence to believe in Your ability to work miracles in my heart today. In the name of Jesus, Amen.

Daily Rhythms

It seems like the world offers us only two kinds of relationships: people we agree with and people we don't. People we agree with are good, righteous, and God-fearing; people we don't agree with are bad, wicked, and bound for the underground! But in reality, God makes it clear that we will have differences with others—in personality, in outlook, and even in faith. The real challenge is deciding what we will do with those differences. Will you allow differences to divide you, or will you overcome them and unite? The choice is yours.

Day 1: Every Effort

/\

Bible Reading: ROMANS 14:1-19

One of the most important things we can understand in the Christian life is exactly *what* God requires of us. As we look at a passage from Romans today, some context: Paul spends twelve chapters earlier in this letter to the Romans making sure his readers understand the glorious goodness of grace, which works within us to transform us to be more like Christ. In view of that grace, he offers instructions for godly living with one another. One of the arguments between the new believers in Rome was about food and drink. Now we might scoff at what these believers were fighting about, but consider some of the current public fighting happening in (and outside) the church:

- politics
- the role of women in ministry
- race and racial reconciliation
- worship styles in services
- human sexuality

Now, you might think, *Nicole, these are big issues! We have to engage with what matters.* But I will tell you—the argument going on in Rome when Paul was writing his letter was a big deal to them. It was a matter of salvation. It was about how their actions impacted their public witness. It was about change, loyalty, and trust. So as you read Paul's instructions, remember that they are applicable for you, right where you are, in the issues you are confronting at home, work, and church. Let's take a closer look at what the passage has to say about God-honoring relationships. This series of quick-fire short answers add up to a lifestyle in Christ:

1. In verse 7, are we called to be independent or interdependent on each other?

2. In verse 12, who will give a personal account before God?

3. In verse 13, what are we called to do for our brother or sister?

4. In verse 16, what are we supposed to stand up for?

5. In verse 19, what are we working toward?

Notice the healthy and very real tension that exists in these verses. We are called to be dependent on one another, but we will all give account for our own actions. We are called to not put any stumbling blocks in the way of others, but also to speak up for what we know is good. We are called to choose peace, but we have to work for it. This is a true tension. It isn't easy or black-and-white. This isn't about a set of rules. It's about a vision of a way to live with other people.

If it feels impossible, that's because it is. It is absolutely impossible to live into this vision without the Spirit of God. We must feel the weight of this way of life without Christ, and then open ourselves up to allow God to lead us into this way of living, one step at a time.

Let's take a closer look at our memory Scripture for the week, Romans 14:19, in three different translations. Underline the "action phrase" in each verse. I've done the first one for you:

Let us therefore <u>make every effort</u> to do what leads to peace and to mutual edification.
NIV

Let us pursue what makes for peace and for mutual upbuilding.
ESV

Let us pursue [with enthusiasm] the things which make for peace and the building up of one another [things which lead to spiritual growth].
AMP

6. What would "making every effort" look like for you in a relationship this week?

When we talk about peace, we aren't referring to a false emotional cease-fire or a "let's just pretend this didn't happen" kind of peace. In fact, God condemns this kind of peace:

Prophets and priests alike,
    all practice deceit.
They dress the wound of my people
    as though it were not serious.
"Peace, peace," they say,
    when there is no peace.
JEREMIAH 6:13-14

God calls it *deceitful* to pretend there is peace when peace has not actually been pursued.

Meditation Moment

Are you tempted to choose false peace? If so, spend a few minutes bringing your fears or disbelief before God and ask Him to meet you there. The apostle Paul tells us that God Himself, through Christ, is "our peace" (Ephesians 2:14). When we find our peace in Him, we discover the strength and courage to try again to choose love and vulnerability in our relationships.

Consider this prayer for your closing minutes with God today as you breathe in and exhale fully into the truth based on 1 Peter 5:7, Colossians 3:15, and Romans 14:19:

> *God, I cast my cares upon You*
> *because You care for me.*
>
> *Jesus, I choose to accept*
> *Your peace as my peace.*
>
> *I choose to make every effort toward peace today.*
> *I choose thankfulness over discouragement.*
> *I choose hope over despair.*
> *I choose trust over defeat.*
>
> *Amen.*

Day 2: Assessing the Breach

Bible Reading: JOHN 21:15-25

Let's return to the relationship between Jesus and Peter in John 21. In the person of Jesus, we see perfect reconciliation modeled. In this passage with Peter, we see the incredible transformation that happens when people pursue forgiveness, reconciliation, and repentance. However, it is equally important to remember that although Jesus offers reconciliation to all, not everyone will accept it. He offers the rich young ruler an action step to follow Him, and the ruler turns away sad (Mark 10:21-22). As Jesus taught, many of His disciples "turned back and no longer followed him" (John 6:66). Jesus offers a new way of living, but it is an offer, not a demand. Although forgiveness in Christ is a free gift for those who will receive it (Revelation 22:17), only those who enter into the classroom of life with Jesus will experience the fullness of the fruit of the Spirit manifested in their lives.

Still, we can choose to pursue forgiveness, reconciliation, and repentance as we strive to love one another. Let's look at how Scripture describes this process.

1. **Forgiveness:** Read Ephesians 4:32. Because Christ has forgiven us, what are we required to do with one another?

   a.

   b.

   c.

2. **Reconciliation:** Forgiveness is a one-way street. We offer forgiveness because Christ forgave us, regardless of how the one who offended us responds. However, reconciliation is a two-way street, requiring both parties to desire and commit to moving forward. Forgiveness is what releases our heart from the power of hurt. Reconciliation is possible only when a relationship can be restored because each person is committed to it.

Read Titus 3:9-10. In your own words, what does this tell you about the commitment required from both people in order to reconcile?

3. **Repentance** (in the original Greek *metanoeō*—"to change the orientation of the mind"): To repent in the biblical context is "to undergo a moral reorientation of the soul in which one acknowledges the error of his ways and turns toward . . . truth and righteousness."[1] Repentance requires a change of mind and a change of action. Although we can experience full freedom in Christ through forgiveness, reconciliation in relationships is not fully realized without repentance.

   Write out Matthew 3:8. What kind of fruit is evidence of repentance? (Check Galatians 5:22-23; John 15:4; Ephesians 5:9; and James 3:17.)

4. Now turn to Acts 3:19 for some good news! What does God promise comes with repentance?

5. What's the difference between receiving or offering an apology and experiencing reconciliation and repentance? What does it do for the relationship?

Meditation Moment

Friends, we are in pro-level relationship work when we begin to pursue not just forgiveness, not just "making nice," but truly making every effort to seek real peace in our relationships. What's important to remember is that God does not call us to "be perfect at achieving peace"; He calls us to "make every effort" at it. We practice, but we won't be perfect. As you come close to Jesus for these few minutes, consider a way you want to "make every effort" toward peace today. Is there a thinking pattern you need to cultivate? An action you need to take? Write down any reflections from your quiet space today:

Day 3: Let Your Yes Be Yes

Bible Reading: JOHN 15:16-17; 2 CORINTHIANS 13:11

In Jesus' greatest sermon, the Sermon on the Mount, He lays out a way of life in the Kingdom of God. Found in Matthew 5–7, this teaching centers on a Kingdom of humility, a place where it's possible to give generously, to love even those who hate us, to experience forgiveness and goodness even when the world offers darkness. Jesus teaches us that what happens in the interior of our hearts is paramount, and that from our heart will flow a sacrificial love for others.

Jesus calls us to a life of integrity, aligning our heart with our words and actions. Matthew 5:37 says, "Let what you say be simply 'Yes' or 'No'" (ESV).

Pursuing connection and reconciliation in relationships starts with the way we orient our own hearts. It is not our responsibility to change others, but to come to Jesus, hear His words, and put them into practice (Matthew 7:24). We do this out of obedience to Him, not in an attempt to control the outcome.

1. In John 15:16-17, why does Jesus say that He's given us His commands?

2. Jesus calls us to integrity with our words because that's the way we show love to one another. Read James 4:17. What qualifies as sin?

You might be thinking that this is a pretty simple lesson . . . but sometimes simple truth can be difficult to execute! My challenge for you today is to pay attention to any time you are tempted to sin—or, as James says, to know what you ought to do and then not do it. In addition, pay attention to any time you are tempted to stretch, manipulate, or avoid the truth. To do so is to damage your witness as a follower of Jesus.

Remember, this exercise is not designed to make you feel bad about yourself. On the contrary, applying Jesus' law brings us into proper placement with our heavenly Father. When we experience God's mercy, we grow in our mercy toward others.

3. What does Mark 5:19 say to do after we have experienced God's forgiveness in our own weakness and sin?

 ## Meditation Moment

Reflect on your patterns of avoiding the truth. Are there circumstances or people in your life with whom it is harder to have integrity? Spend time asking God to enlighten your heart to understand your own broken ways of handling your sin, and ask Him to strengthen you in His love and purpose.

Day 4: Action Plans

Bible Reading: JOHN 21:15-22

Yesterday we learned that rebuilding trust after a relationship rupture doesn't happen just through words—it requires action. Let's turn again to the passage with Jesus and Peter and learn what true repentance looks like.

1. Reread John 21:15-22. Note here what actions Jesus calls Peter to do. (I'll complete the first one for you.)

   verse 15: feed my lambs

   verse 16:

   verse 17:

   verse 22:

For every one of Peter's betrayals on the night Jesus was arrested, Jesus repairs the breach. For every curse, Jesus gives Peter the opportunity to rebuild with love. Jesus has just demonstrated His love and forgiveness for the world in His death—and His power to overcome the world in His resurrection. Now He engages with Peter in a personal, direct, and intimate way to repair the breach between them. Notice that Jesus does not want Peter to apologize with words or to grovel before Him. He just calls him to action and to step into the fullness of who he can be—and who he already is—because of his relationship with Jesus.

2. Now, fast-forward in Peter's life and read Acts 2:38-47. What is the fruit of Peter's commitment to Jesus? Jot down what is happening around Peter's leadership at the time:

Truly, Peter is embodying exactly what Jesus called him to: his role as a leader of the flock of believers and his commitment to follow Christ. He doesn't do it perfectly (read Acts 10:9-48 about another time Jesus reinstates Peter to his calling!), but he keeps repenting and growing.

3. Now turn to James 1:22-25. What happens to those who listen to the Word of God but don't do anything about it?

When it comes to God's command that we make every effort toward peace, we can't just use words to get there—we have to act. This includes naming the offense and forgiving (releasing the past), identifying actions that symbolize a desire to rebuild in the present, and then letting those actions be steps in our walk toward the future. What we do today won't necessarily heal everything that's gone wrong. But in the relationship, we commit to saying, "This action represents me wanting to rebuild."

Let me use an example to illustrate. I am sometimes absent-minded about my schedule, particularly when it comes to social engagements. I have one friend who is more concrete and future-oriented, so if I say, "Let's do something next weekend," she may interpret that to mean we have firm plans.

Recently, we had a conflict because of this problem. She thought we had made plans; I didn't think we had committed to those plans. She interpreted that as a lack of commitment to our relationship; I interpreted her hurt as lack of trust in my intentions. At this point, we could "play nice" and pretend that nothing had transpired between us, or we could lean into reconciliation. A miracle moment would be possible once we recognized that our individual interpretations were leading to resentment, which resulted in a growing distance between us. Initiating a miracle moment meant making the courageous choice to address this resentment directly rather than allowing it to simmer under the surface.

Reconciliation between my friend and me looked like this:

Seek to understand: We had a sincere desire to hear each other out and honor the other person's experience.

Seek the common good: We reiterated our desire to be in a friendship and to work it out.

Seek restoration: Each of us needed to ask the other, "How will I know you are committed to changing?" For my part, I promised that the next time we had plans, I would be more specific and detailed. She promised that the next time we had plans, she would reach out and confirm to ensure we were on the same page.

Our reconciliation required action. No matter how small, a breach of trust is still a breach. Committing to specific steps is a way to symbolize our mutual desire to connect, not distance ourselves through the conflict.

Will we always do it perfectly? No way. But are we making a sincere, concerted effort to "bear fruit in keeping with repentance" (Matthew 3:8, esv)? Yes. And mutually vulnerable, mutually committed, mutually beneficial relationships require this level of engagement.

Meditation Moment

Many times on this journey, we may find ourselves remembering a relationship that did not go well or was not mutually loving or connected. Such memories may tempt us to believe that miracle moments aren't possible—or at least not for us.

If you find yourself ruminating about a failed or broken relationship, I want you to take heart and know that *miracles are still real for you.* I want to invite you to bring that broken, failed, unreconciled, or confusing relationship to God and let Him be in it with you. This promise is true for you: "If anyone is in Christ, he/she is a new creation. The old has gone, the new has come!" (see 2 Corinthians 5:17). Even if your broken relationship happened while you were "in Christ," it does not disqualify you from new life. Today is a day when you can believe again that a new start is possible, that miracles do happen, and that God wants to heal you from that past relationship so it no longer has power over your present or future.

Spend these minutes simply enjoying the healing presence of God, knowing that He does not need you to be anyone other than who you are. He doesn't need you to be put together, peaceful, confident, or even good. He just desires to heal you, care for you, and lead you through this day.

Write down any reflections from this time below:

Day 5: A Boundaries Intro

/\

Bible Reading: MARK 3:20-35

Boundaries will be the main topic of our study next week, but even this week it's impossible to talk about reconciliation without mentioning boundaries. Our personal boundaries are both protective and proactive. They are *protective* when they keep the bad out—they help us understand how to live in a way that allows us to be obedient to Christ, especially with those who don't honor or respect those boundaries. Boundaries are also *proactive*—they are intentional commitments we make to ourselves that allow us to live into our purpose in the world.

Ultimately, healthy boundaries are God-honoring. They are required to keep us focused on God's design for our lives and to make the choices necessary to live into our calling as "citizens of heaven" (Philippians 3:20, NLT).

Let's look at how Jesus modeled healthy boundaries for us during His earthly life as we read Mark 3:20-35.

1. What do Jesus' mother and brothers believe about His lifestyle?

2. What do the teachers of the law believe about Jesus' lifestyle?

3. What does Jesus say about His purpose (Mark 2:10, 17, 28)?

If nothing else, this short study reveals one thing: Jesus is consistently misunderstood, even by the people who are presumably closest to him. They try to interpret His life for Him and then try to control Him through their own influence. And true to our own experience, it is often the people who've known us our whole lives that have the hardest time respecting our boundaries.

4. Have you ever been misunderstood by people in your life, even when you were endeavoring to honor God? Have you ever felt . . .

   a. a sense of disappointment from family or friends when you haven't done what they wanted you to do, even though you never agreed to what they wanted?

   b. anger or frustration in a relationship because a person wanted you to live up to an unstated expectation?

   c. frustration at a person who doesn't listen or take action on what you think would be best for their life?

If you answered yes to one (or all three!) of these statements, you've experienced a boundary violation. Reflect on the following passage:

One of the misconceptions people have about boundaries is that they are inherently selfish or lead to loneliness or isolation. Nothing could be further from the truth. Knowing and living by your boundaries allows you to express love—not out of resentment or obligation, but out of generosity and freedom. Boundaries allow you to use your resources in a way that aligns with your purpose and values, rather than feeling that you have to live your life by other people's standards.

THE MIRACLE MOMENT, CHAPTER 9, PAGE 168

5. Have you ever felt compelled to live by other people's standards? What is your general response to feeling controlled, influenced, or manipulated by the judgments of others?

Jesus is our perfect example of what it looks like to live completely committed to God's boundaries for a life—and as it turns out, it is not a life free from conflict, suffering, or struggle! Yet Jesus knew perfect love, perfect peace, and perfect joy in obedience to His Father, and He invites us to the same.

One of the ways we become committed to God's authority for our boundaries is to continue to rehearse God's goodness to us. The more we trust God with our lives, the more courageous we can be with our boundaries.

6. Read Psalm 16:5-8. Fill in the following list of what God does in these verses, and what we do in our personal relationship with Him:

God's job	My job

 Meditation Moment

God's job is to be our counsel. He is the one who sets out the boundaries of our lives, our families, our friendships, and our work. As an exercise in trust, spend five minutes thinking of the "pleasant places" God has provided for you. Feel free to use the space below to record some of them (relationships, opportunities, or insights).

AN INVITATION TO INTEGRITY

ᨆᨆᨆᨆ

*Love and trust are two different things. We can love people for their
inherent worth, but trust is earned over time. And when we see yellow-
light indicators, we should slow down and test the waters before jumping
in with both feet. When we are self-aware and follow the steps for deeper
relationship and conversation, we are inviting people to take off their armor
and grow in connection and vulnerability. It's an invitation—not a mandate.*

The Miracle Moment, *chapter 10, page 196*

ᨆᨆᨆᨆ

This Week's Recommended Reading:
Chapters 10 and 11 in *The Miracle Moment*

WE BEGAN THIS journey together by asking an audacious question: "Are miracles possible in our relationships?" We've committed to allow Jesus to be
the teacher in the classroom of life. We've begun to practice the lessons Jesus
teaches about developing our self-awareness (mean what we feel) and our self-
expression (say what we mean). Now we will learn how to align our emotions
and words with our actions (do what we say). Following through on our words
with our deeds is what makes us trustworthy and safe people. And safety is
what enables us to choose love over fear and connection over conflict.

Integrity is the alignment of emotions, words, and actions in the
pursuit of a God-honoring life.

Tune in to video session 6: "An Invitation to Integrity."

Video Notes

Boundaries create the freedom needed to be compelled by love
(2 Corinthians 5:14).

Integrity allows you to share not only the gospel but your life as well
(1 Thessalonians 2:8).

A person is safe or not by his or her ability to _____ empathy,
to _____ honesty, and to _____ on repentance.

Hope is trusting God for the outcome.

 ## A Moment of Reflection

Setting boundaries is critical if we are to love ourselves and others well. By clarifying our limits, responsibilities, and preferences, we are free to offer safety and compassion to others without violating our own well-being. While boundaries serve as a hedge of protection, they are not meant to be rigid and unyielding. They are, however, intended to help us navigate relationships in healthy ways.

DO YOU HAVE HEALTHY BOUNDARIES?

The following assessment gives you a quick check on the extent of healthy boundaries in your life.

Boundaries Assessment

Answer yes or no to each statement. Don't think too long; just answer from your gut.

1. My closest relationships tend to be conflictual, drama laden, or controlling. _____

2. I often struggle to make decisions. _____

3. Sometimes I'm not sure what I really want. _____

4. I often feel guilty, fearful, or worried that I am letting people down. _____

5. Sometimes I feel like a doormat to the people in my life I'm closest to. _____

6. I avoid being alone. _____

7. I sometimes don't know how to share or be vulnerable—or with whom. _____

8. I am secretly resentful toward some loved ones in my life who've taken advantage of my kindness. _____

9. I've been accused of being passive-aggressive. _____

10. I find it very difficult to say no to certain people in my life. _____

11. I don't like to share my opinion when it differs from that of the people I respect. _____

12. When I do finally share my thoughts, I have a hard time knowing if I'm sharing too much. _____

13. Sometimes I'm tempted to get as much as I can from another person to keep them close. _____

14. Sometimes I'm compelled to give more than I can to another person so I don't lose them. _____

15. I would rather take care of others' needs than take care of myself. _____

Scoring this assessment

Every one of these questions indicates a potential boundary issue. The more times you've answered yes, the more likely it is that you are having a hard time knowing and enforcing your boundaries. But even one yes is worth paying attention to. Think of the issue or relationship that comes to mind as you consider how to communicate and enforce boundaries.

Having assessed your own boundaries, consider the following questions:

1. Why are boundaries important to your ability to share the gospel by the way you live?

2. What qualities in others help you feel safe with them?

3. Which qualities in yourself do you believe help others feel safe with you? In what areas do you want to grow?

In the Word

Let's look more closely at the conflict in the early church from the video teaching.

1. What dispute had developed between believers (Acts 15:1, 5)?

2. Acts 15:1-33 is a study in healthy conflict negotiation. What do you observe in the passage that leads to a successful resolution?

3. In Acts 15:36-41, we see an unexpected twist to the story. What happens?

4. Turn to 2 Timothy 4:11 for a hint at how the dispute between John Mark and Paul might have been resolved. Likely, almost fifteen years pass between the Council at Jerusalem (AD 48 or 49) and the writing of the letter we call 2 Timothy (AD 64 or 65). What causes Paul to trust John Mark again?

Application

1. These Scripture passages are a window into the human side of us all—the vulnerability, the mistakes, and the failures. What qualities do you look for in people to determine whether they are trustworthy?

2. As you think about a resolution recorded in Scripture fifteen years after the original dispute, are you more or less hopeful for your own miracle moments? Is your tendency to hang on too long or give up too quickly on a failed, stuck, or conflicted relationship?

3. Have you had an experience where you've loved someone but not trusted them? What's the difference between love and trust?

We close our time today returning to the fifth law of miracles: *Hope makes change possible.* As you reflect on how you are experiencing God through this study, in what areas has He restored your hope? What *small is big* changes have you experienced in yourself? What miracles are you hoping for in your life? Take a moment to record some of the experiences you've had as evidence of the Spirit's work in your life.

 ## Memory Moment
This week's memory moment is from the book of Micah:

> What does the LORD require of you?
> To act justly and to love mercy
>   and to walk humbly with your God.
> MICAH 6:8

Closing Prayer

My heavenly Father, You are the God of hope. Jesus, You are Lord of all, and You are Lord over every relationship, every obstacle, and every hurt in my heart. Spirit, You give me the power to be obedient to Your call to love. I specifically thank You for the ways I've seen You work in my life this week:

God, I pray that I would not take these miracles for granted. Sink Your truths deep into my heart, that no matter what season I find myself in, I know Your love and grace for me. Amen.

 Daily Rhythms

I hope by this time in our study, you've begun to see that miracles are possible—particularly the kind of miracle that happens within us—in the way we grow in our awareness of our own actions and reactions and in the way we empathize with and forgive others. But this week, we are dealing with another reality of our world: that we do (and will) have trouble. We cannot escape trouble in our relationships. Throughout Scripture, God struggled with His chosen people (Exodus 32); Jesus struggled with His followers (Matthew 23:37), and the apostle Paul struggled with himself! (Romans 7:15-19). Integrity isn't about becoming struggle-free—it's about having the proper perspective within the struggle.

Day 1: Do What You Say

Bible Reading: ESTHER 4:10–5:3

Conviction is a moment of opportunity and decision. When confronted with truth, how will we respond? Today we are looking at one of the most courageous people in the Bible as our inspiration for action: Esther.

A little backstory: Esther was a Jewish orphan-turned-queen during the reign of Xerxes in the ancient kingdom of Persia. Although she rose to royal status because of her beauty and character, she didn't share power with the king (see Esther 1:9-22 to learn what happened to the queen before Esther).

1. Read Esther 4:10-17. What does Mordecai say to convict Esther, leading her to risk her life for her people (verse 14)?

2. What excuses does Esther give Mordecai as to why she doesn't want to act (verses 10-11)?

3. What steps does Esther eventually take after Mordecai's confrontation?

Esther's moment of courage—when she aligns her heart, words, and actions—eventually leads to the downfall of the king's advisor, Haman, who has been conspiring to annihilate all of the Jewish people in the kingdom. Esther's shrewd plan and bold faith impact an entire generation.

Now think about your own life. You may not be faced with a decision as weighty as Esther's, but all of us have the choice either to step into our lives with courage or to shrink back in fear. Boundaries aren't about self-protection or self-centeredness. Rather, they create the space we need to know *who we are* and *what we are worth*, and to say yes and no to the right things so we can live out our calling fully.

It may seem unusual to choose the story of Esther to illustrate boundaries. But that's exactly why I chose it. Esther represents *a self-defined individual with a non-anxious presence.*[1] With the help of Mordecai, she is able to see her own power and use it for the sake of others. That's what boundaries do. They allow us to act with conviction based on the love we desire to see in ourselves and in the world. They create space for miracle moments—when we can step into relationships with vulnerability, name our needs or desires, and stand by the steps we need to take to honor ourselves—and others.

4. Review your boundaries assessment from this week's lesson. What areas may be holding you back from positioning yourself to step into your relationships with grace and truth?

5. Imagine yourself being free of those issues for one day. What would be different about you if you weren't living out of that pattern?

Understanding, creating, and enforcing boundaries is a new idea for many people and requires time to learn and practice. Review chapter 9 in *The Miracle Moment* for more on boundaries and how to implement them.

Meditation Moment

What would it look like to love more courageously in one of your relationships? Would it involve a confrontation? More trust? More vulnerability? Take a few minutes to open your heart to a specific action—big or small—that the Spirit is inviting you to "for such a time as this." Stay disciplined in your quiet space with God, and then record any reflections or insights here:

Day 2: Safe People, Part 1

Bible Reading: GENESIS 2:15-25

The culmination of learning to mean what we feel, say what we mean, and do what we say is becoming people of integrity. But not everyone in our lives will be willing to take the same journey. Let's look at the qualities in people that allow for miracle moments—both in themselves and in the safety they create for others.

To be "safe" isn't about protection from physical harm only. Safety is also an emotional and spiritual experience, a connection that allows people to trust one another with vulnerability. Such safety and mutual connection was the original design of humanity.

Answer the following questions that relate to today's Bible reading.

1. What did God create man to do?

2. What did God decide was "not good"?

3. How does verse 25 describe the connection between the man and woman?

In our pre-sin state, we were designed for full vulnerability (nakedness) and full connection.

4. Read Genesis 3:7-10. What happened after Adam and Eve sinned?

In this original account of humanity, we see that God created us for full, unashamed openness and connection—but the first thing sin did was create shame. And shame always leads to fear and evasion. To be a safe person is to be willing to come out of hiding and offer those around you the security to do the same.

Tomorrow, we'll look at three hallmark qualities of safe people: honesty, empathy, and repentance.

 ## Meditation Moment

Psalm 112:4 says, "Even in darkness light dawns for the upright." As you seek to live with integrity, what light is God shining into your story right now? Are there parts of your life you've been trying to hide in the dark? Spend time with God and allow whatever hurt, shame, or fear might be lurking in the shadows to come into the presence of His healing, compassionate, and gracious light.

Day 3: Safe People, Part 2

Bible Reading: 1 PETER 3:8-16

Discernment is the ability to know good from evil, light from darkness. Jesus repeatedly warns His followers to watch out for false teaching, for deceivers and hypocrites, and for insidious beliefs that infect a whole community (Matthew 7:15; 24:4; Mark 8:15). Discernment is the ability to see good and evil in others—as well as in ourselves. As we strive to become safe people, we will be better able to recognize those who are unsafe or unwilling to change.

There are three essential qualities in people that create safety and the capacity for intimacy and connection:

Honesty: Safe people are able to speak truthfully about their experiences and the experiences of others, both positive and negative.

1. Read 1 Chronicles 29:17. King David is offering a blessing to the people as he passes the scepter to his son Solomon. He acknowledges the Lord's sovereignty and ability to test our hearts. Sometimes the idea of being honest before God or other people can be intimidating—especially when we realize we have an enormous capacity to deceive ourselves! But what phrase does King David use to describe the position of his heart in this verse?

Empathy: Safe people are able to engage emotionally with the experiences of other people.

2. Read 1 Peter 3:8-16. List the instructions that reflect the quality of engaging emotionally with others. (There are several! List the three to five that resonate most with you today.)

Repentance: Safe people are able to own their faults and mistakes, apologize to those they've wronged or with whom they've violated trust, and "turn around" (the root of the word *repent* is "to turn") with their words *and* actions, including seeking help when necessary.

3. Read Hebrews 3:12-13. What does "sin's deceitfulness" do in you? What are you tempted to believe when your heart is turned away from God? Think back to your emotional reactions and fear triggers from sessions 3 and 4.

4. Do you agree that the qualities of a safe person are honesty, empathy, and repentance? Would you add any qualities to this list? If so, which ones?

Meditation Moment

Like King David, we can enter into conversation with God, confessing our willingness and "honest intent" to come to Him and to grow into a safe person. When you think about the qualities of honesty, empathy, and repentance, where have you seen growth in your life, and where do you think God is prompting more growth in you?

Thank God for the work He's already done in your heart, and affirm your commitment to the work He continues to do.

Day 4: When It Doesn't Get Better:
Dealing with Relational Pain

Bible Reading: GALATIANS 5:1; TITUS 3:10-11

It is tempting to believe that if we do everything right, we can make any relationship work. But sometimes even our best efforts don't seem to improve a relationship. All the self-awareness and empathy in the world don't work when the other person won't (or can't) change.

> What's funny about our boundaries is that when we are in unhealthy relationships, we desperately want approval and validation *from those same unsafe people* for our healthy choices. But people who have benefited from our inability to stand up for ourselves will not be happy when we begin setting limits. They will be frustrated, hurt, and confused by those boundaries, particularly if they are close family members or friends. If we've been living by their expectations, they may find it disconcerting when we change the rules.
> *THE MIRACLE MOMENT*, CHAPTER 10, PAGES 200-201

Let's look at how God can meet us, even when a relationship doesn't turn out the way we planned.

1. Read Galatians 5:1. God calls us to live free and not become enslaved again. In what ways can you become "enslaved" in your relationships?

2. Turn to Titus 2:11-12. What does the grace of God—the way we live in freedom—do for us?

3. Now turn to 2 Timothy 3:1-5. What characteristics describe those who have "a form of godliness" without its power? What is Paul's instruction on how to handle these people?

4. If you've ever loved an unsafe person (someone unwilling or unable to be honest, empathetic, or repentant), you know how difficult it can be to balance your desire to love them with your desire to see them get well. What is your general response to unsafe people?

    a. I distance myself from them, including family members if necessary.

    b. I want to double down on my love for them. I often feel like such people have been hurt and need more healthy relationships in their life.

    c. I vacillate between being frustrated and distant, or compassionate and wanting to help them make better decisions.

    d. I have trouble even knowing whether someone is safe or unsafe.

    e. Other:_____

Once again, there is no right answer to the above question. These prompts are designed to help you get more in touch with your own emotional triggers and increase your self-awareness about any boundary issues you have with people who are not able or willing to pursue healthy relationships.

Of course, the Bible is not instructing us to cut every unsafe person out of our lives—in many ways, we ourselves often "armor up" in relationships and can be unsafe too! But Scripture does illustrate that there are people who are not willing to grow, and there will always be limits to the level of intimacy and connection we will experience with those people. Chapter 10 in *The Miracle Moment* gives more details on how to identify unsafe people and continue to grow ourselves, even in such relationships.

Almost everyone I know has experienced a painful relational failure (most just don't talk about it). Failures, breakups, and losses of all kinds can create significant wounding. They can shake our foundation in destructive ways. But in God's hands, failure can also be a great teacher, helping us learn humility, compassion, and resilience.

5. Turn to Isaiah 43:18-19. What does God promise He's able to do?

 ## Meditation Moment

"See, I am doing a new thing!" (Isaiah 43:19). Take a few minutes to read through the Isaiah passage several times, out loud if possible. Listen for the truth, knowing that God's sense of our life is set in eternity, not this month, this year, or even this decade. Let yourself breathe in the truth and hopefulness of this passage, while making space for any part of you that's angry, frustrated, or confused about things that are not healed or reconciled in your life. If you do discover some underlying hurt there, bring it into your awareness and ask the Spirit of God to give you insight.

Day 5: Unshakable Hope

Bible Reading: GALATIANS 3:2-6

I can think of no better place to conclude our journey together than in this powerful statement from Galatians. The truth is that the journey of our faith is never over. It is a progressive experience of the miracle of hope, of connection, of death and resurrection.

1. Read Galatians 3:2-6. Write down the five questions Paul asks.

   a.

   b.

   c.

   d.

   e.

   These questions point us to a mindset that we are all tempted to live from: a commitment to rational experience over spiritual belief.

2. According to verse 6, what is the source of our righteousness?

3. As you reflect on your takeaways from this study, what do you need to keep believing God for in your life?

4. What law of miracles do you need to believe in order to continue to have "eyes to see" God's work in your relationships?

5. What limiting or damaging mindset or belief do you need to guard your heart from?

6. In which area do you want to commit to continued growth?

    a. my ability to seek to understand, assume positive intent, and own all that I can

    b. my self-awareness around the ways I live from fear, and my empathy and discernment for fear triggers in others

    c. my commitment to rebuilding trust in relationships after conflict

    d. my engagement with and enforcing of healthy boundaries in my life

    e. my openness to healing and forgiveness in the painful parts of my past or present and my refusal to allow those wounds to define my existence

    f. other: _____

Meditation Moment

Friend, my deepest desire is that the space you've created to draw near to God over these past weeks has become a refuge of safety, comfort, healing, and peace for you. If you take away nothing else from this study, I pray that you will be forever changed by the five minutes of meditation with God each day. I urge you to cling to this habit moving forward. The Spirit of God works powerfully within us, even in ways we cannot discern (Romans 8:26-27). In the joy and in the pain, the Spirit of God is the miracle worker in both the interior of our souls and the exterior of our relationships. For your final meditation of this study, I invite you to write a prayer of thanksgiving to God for the miracles He is working in your life.

A Final Blessing

AS WE REACH the end of our journey through this video series and Bible study, my hope is that you've begun to experience the miracle moments all around you. Although these miracles often come within uncomfortable scenarios, they also come with great promise. By now I hope you've begun to uncover patterns that might be limiting your freedom and joy. But the real miracle comes from what you do *next*.

Once you understand that Jesus is not only your Good Shepherd and sovereign Savior, but He is also your daily *Teacher*, you'll know that your faith is growing and that miracles are possible. And when a miracle moment comes—the moment you recognize that you were *just about* to react as you normally do but instead allow God to give you the patience and perseverance to choose love, humility, or patience—then you'll know that you've been changed. You'll know that you can testify to the very present reality of our loving God who still works miracles today. I would love to leave you with this blessing as we conclude our work together:

And now . . .
May the God of Creation create a new heart in you.

May you accept Jesus as your wise teacher,
your only Savior,
and your closest friend.

May the gift of the Spirit
dwell richly,
fully,
and joyfully within you.

And may you experience miracles
all around you,
past, present, and future . . .
beyond your wildest imagination.

A Guide for Leaders

CAN I LET YOU in on a little secret? You are perfectly equipped to lead your group.

I know, I know! You might feel unworthy, unprepared, or even apathetic about leading this group. Your own faith may feel as stale as week-old bread. Your own relationships may feel shakier or more fractured than you would like to admit. But you've been called to this moment, to these people, for this time of learning. You are in good company. Jesus had barely even given His seventy-two disciples His blessing before He sent them out to minister. (See Luke 10:1—in addition to his closest twelve, there were seventy-two more!) I think God delights in putting us in situations that we aren't ready to handle—so we won't forget our need for Him. His grace is sufficient, and He will provide what you need.

Now send out those invites—you are officially in ministry. One more thing: Leaders aren't immune from insight, growth, and miracles. God has called you as the leader of this group because that positioning is your calling in the body of Christ. Your leadership makes you more like Jesus—not because leaders are special, but because in your life, God has gifted you and called you to grow specifically when you are in leadership roles. So hold tightly to the confidence of the calling, but also hold on tight—because God is as interested in your miracle moments as He is for those in everyone in your group!

This guide will help you with the resources you need to launch and lead your group. On the next page, you'll find answers to the questions leaders often ask, followed by leaders' notes for each session.

Who should be in my group?

There is no perfect formula for a group. Any context that draws people together can be the basis for forming one. For you, this might look like an existing Bible study or Sunday school class. My hope is that it might look like a group of friends you usually work out with, a gathering of coworkers, or the moms from your child's soccer team. If some activity or group of people draws you together, you already have something in common.

The Miracle Moment is written for anyone who wants to know how to use conflict in their life as a tool for deeper connection rather than division. Some questions and inventories will invite your group to be vulnerable, but we've structured each session to give you multiple entry points—and sharing is always optional. So everyone is welcome, and hopefully there's a little bit of something for everyone in the study!

What do we need to get started?

Everyone in the group needs a copy of this participant's guide and a Bible for group time. We also recommend that members pick up a copy of *The Miracle Moment*, but it is not required for the study.

How long will each group session take?

The study is structured so that each session can be completed in ninety minutes. If you have less time, you can edit the questions and choose to move more of the group work to personal study time. Here is the suggested format:

10 minutes: Welcome and Connection Question
10 minutes: Observations from Previous Session's Daily Study
20 minutes: Video Time
10 minutes: Reflection
20 minutes: In the Word
15 minutes: Application
5 minutes: Prayer

I don't know how to be a leader. Help!

If you are new to facilitating a group, rest assured that you are not alone. Everyone is intimidated when they first start leading a group. It can feel presumptuous to pretend that you are the spiritually mature one who is ready to "lead" your peers in Bible study! But have no fear—that's not the spirit of this study.

A great group leader doesn't need to have all the answers (in fact, that usually makes a person *not* a great leader). A great group leader does two things. One, the leader makes the group *safe*. *Safe* means the leader starts and ends on time, keeps the group on track with questions, and gently redirects if one group member is trying to give advice or "fix" someone else. Second, the leader models *honesty* by a willingness to be vulnerable when responding to the questions, creating space for people to share fully and openly, and encouraging each member of the group to grow. A group that has both safety and honesty is a setting where powerful development can happen.

Here are some other helpful hints as you lead your group:

- This study works equally well in a ministry setting, such as a larger group situated around tables, or in a home or small group setting.

- As the leader, you set the tone for the depth and authenticity of your group. Your job is not to have all the answers, but to be open so that people can come with questions and vulnerability and feel heard and understood. You do that by sharing from your own life and by giving others the space to share.

- You also set the tone through your own preparation. By previewing the video and working through the questions in the guide in advance, you'll have a better sense of what questions to focus on and how the group is likely to go each time you meet. Your preparation also tells your group that you value their time and expect this experience to be important and meaningful. Be sure to preview this leader's guide each week before the group meets in case you need extra materials or preparation. The tone of the leader determines the tone of the group.

- Communication as a leader is key. Make sure you connect with your group between sessions via email, text, etc., to clarify what the group should do to prepare for the next meeting and to remind them when and where you'll be meeting.

- Your group will most likely not have time to respond to every question during your time together—and that's OK! The questions fit into three categories: connecting with one another, knowing the Word, and applying the Word to life. Depending on the experiences of the people in the group, some of those categories may be more conducive to discussion than others. Try to hit at least one of the questions from each section every time you meet, but focus on what's best for your group.

- Remember that you can refer to the answer key available in the Choose the Miracle Toolkit at nicoleunice.com/miracles if you're unsure about the correct response to any question. You might also remind your group that they can access it as well.

 Session 1

The following guidelines are meant to help you manage your time and get the most out of your group. Remember, these instructions are intended to give you confidence as you get to know your group members and respond to what works best for them. As the weeks go on, you will become more confident about and comfortable with what the group needs.

Session 1 Goal
To establish the rhythm of your group, create a comfortable environment, and make initial connections with one another

Welcome (10 minutes)
Make sure everyone knows one another's names. Go over the basics: stage of life, workplace, what drew the person to the group. Don't forget to share what prompted you to start or lead the group! (Note: For session 1 only, I suggest planning for a slightly extended welcome time to allow for group introductions. In the guidelines for sessions 2 through 6, the Welcome and Connection Question are combined.)

Connection Question (10 minutes)
Even if your group members already know each other well, connection time is a chance to find out something new, to hear something different, and to allow space for old friends to surprise one another with new details. If your group members don't know one another well or at all, this time is *crucial* because it gives everyone a chance to be themselves without the intimidation of jumping right into a conversation about spiritual things. I'll always provide direction, but feel free to make this time your own.

Much of our time together will involve looking back at our lives in order to look forward to our future. As we start, tell us about your first best friend. How did you meet, what did you love doing together, and what did you learn about life from that person?

Video Time (20 minutes)

Tune in to session 1: "Setting Up for a Miracle." Make sure everyone knows they can take notes in their guide as they listen.

Reflection (10 minutes)

Consult session 1 in your guide for questions that follow the video content. You may not be able to answer every one in the time you have, so pick one or two to focus on and then return to this section if you have extra time.

In the Word (20 minutes)

This section is designed to help everyone get comfortable exploring the Bible together. It can be helpful to have an extra Bible handy so you can pass it around and read aloud.

Application (15 minutes)

This is the takeaway—where it gets real. If you run out of time, feel free to share your own answer to the Application question as a way to set a tone of honesty for the group.

Prayer (5 minutes)

In the first session, it's best for you to close in prayer. As you get to know your group, you can move to sharing prayer requests and then praying together. Be mindful of those in your group who are exploring faith or are new to faith. Avoid falling into "Christianese"—the tendency for Christians to use terms that those new to the faith don't understand. Pray sincerely and simply, and you'll help others learn to approach God in the same way.

Don't forget to close your time by covering the basics—when and where you'll meet next, an encouragement to complete the homework, and a reminder to bring a Bible next time. You may wish to get everyone's contact information and follow up with a simple, individual text in the next couple of days. ("Hey, Landon! So glad you joined us for our first group. I really enjoyed what you shared about playing baseball in the street with your first best friend.☺ Looking forward to seeing you next time.")

Simple communication and follow-up will help each person in your group feel known and cared for, which goes a *long* way!

👥 Session 2

Session 2 Goal

To go one level deeper in connection; to become comfortable discussing biblical truths; to share honestly from the homework

Welcome and Connection Question (10 minutes)

Here's a possible question to get your group started:

> **Share about an amazing or terrible group project or team experience you had at school or work, or while volunteering. What made it awesome (or terrible)? What did you accomplish (or not)? How did your experience on that team impact your understanding of yourself?**

Observations from Session 1 Daily Study (10 minutes)

As a way to grow together and stay accountable, open your session with feedback from the week's homework. It can be helpful to give some clear prompts:

> **Let's take a couple of minutes to look back over our notes from last week. Underline any reflection that stuck out for you that you can share.**

This creates an easy way for people to participate without feeling lost in the homework, not sure where to start. This also allows those who could not complete the homework to reflect on the previous video session instead.

Video Time (20 minutes)

Tune in to session 2: "The Heart of the Matter."

Reflection (10 minutes)

Consult session 2 in your guide for questions that follow the video content. Here's a suggested activity:

> Have everyone answer the thinker/feeler inventory. Then, put the thinkers on one side of the room and the feelers on the other. Spend five minutes discussing with your fellow thinkers/feelers what is good about your way of seeing the world and when it can be an obstacle or stumbling block.

In the Word (20 minutes)
This week's content has several verses to look up. Feel free to break those up within the group and then have people share their reflections from each verse. Create a list of promises based on what God says we are worth.

Application (15 minutes)
You may want to generalize the question about beliefs to help the group grow in trust with one another:

> **In your relationships, what beliefs do you think people are tempted to follow that aren't in line with what God's Word says about them? How do you see that impacting you personally?**

Look back at the day 1 homework from session 1. As the leader, share with the group your response to the question, "Do you want to get well?" and then open the floor up for anyone else who wants to state their intentions or hope for their growth during this group.

Prayer (5 minutes)
If your group is ready, this is a great time to pray for one another. You can do this by inviting your group to pair up and share one request that the other person can pray about in the upcoming week. If the group is uncomfortable with that, you could also pick one person to open in prayer and then you could close this prayer time.

It's always helpful to encourage your group to do the homework and remind them of the time and place you'll meet for the next session.

 ## Session 3

Session 3 Goal
To create an environment where it's safe to be a sinner—to define and understand humility and its impact on every relationship in our lives (including with ourselves!)

Welcome and Connection Question (10 minutes)
Here's a possible question to get your group started:

Describe where and when you feel able to be your fullest self. Can you think of a particular experience when you felt free to be open about all parts of you, both the strong and the weak?

Observations from Session 2 Daily Study (10 minutes)

As a way to grow together and stay accountable, open your session with feedback from the week's homework. Your group should be more comfortable now sharing freely.

Looking back on your reflections from last week, what's something new you've discovered about yourself?

Do you have any follow-up comments or questions from our homework last week?

Video Time (20 minutes)

Tune in to session 3: "Humility in Action."

Reflection (10 minutes)

Consult session 3 in your guide for questions that follow the video content. You may not be able to answer every one in the time you have, so pick one or two to focus on and then return to this section if you have extra time.

In the Word (20 minutes)

We are going a bit theological this week with this big idea of humility "becoming us" as creatures, sinners, and saints. Spend some time exploring that idea with your group. It's OK if people have questions or you don't have easy answers.

Application (15 minutes)

Depending on your group's vulnerability, you might want to ask if anyone can share about a memory or moment when their pride blocked them from connection.

Prayer (5 minutes)

As we turn to the practical side of growing in relationships, this could be a good time to pray for difficult relationships. One way to do this that honors people and privacy is to ask folks to write down a specific prayer for a way they want to ask God to work in a difficult relationship, and then seal that prayer in an envelope. You'll return the sealed envelope to them at the end of the study.

It's always helpful to encourage your group to make time to do the upcoming homework. The more engaged your group is in their day-to-day relationships, the more transformative their time with God will become.

🧑‍🤝‍🧑 Session 4

Session 4 Goal
To engage with fear—ours and others'—and see how we can move beyond it to create connection

Welcome and Connection Question (10 minutes)
Here are two questions you can use to get your group started:

As a kid, what were you scared of? Do any of those fears linger today?

What's something that might feel scary to do but you would love to try?

Observations from Session 3 Daily Study (10 minutes)

Look back on your reflections from last week. What did you learn about humility and relationships?

Video Time (20 minutes)
Tune in to session 4: "No Fear in Love."

Reflection (10 minutes)
Consult session 4 in your guide for questions that follow the video content. It will be interesting to hear the group's responses to the conflict style assessment. How are group members alike and different? There is courage in numbers, so if some folks answered similarly, ask them to talk more about their conflict style and how it's been helpful or hurtful to their relationships in the past.

In the Word (20 minutes)
Today we look at the way Mary, Martha, and Jesus interact with one another in the pain of losing Lazarus. Invite conversation around the different ways people engage with pain and how that impacts our ability to connect with each other.

Application (15 minutes)
Discuss the following question with your group:

In what ways could God be using active conflict in your life (within yourself or with others) to draw you closer to Him? Think about the way you feel, the way you speak, and what you believe about yourself and others.

Prayer (5 minutes)

If your group is growing in vulnerability and opening up, you might ask if one or two people want to share about how they are experiencing God in places of fear or pain in their lives. If you are confident in your group's ability to hold confidences and avoid trying to "fix" one another, you might ask if anyone would like the group to pray about a specific situation they feel stuck or paralyzed in. If your group is newer in faith or less ready to share, you could ask each person to take turns reading a verse from a Scripture passage (Psalm 51 or 63 work well) as your closing prayer.

As we move toward our final weeks, encourage your group to continue the habit of working through their daily homework, particularly in spending time each day just being with God in their meditation moment. Remind them to keep an open and attentive mind to the way God is showing up in their past and reshaping their present.

 Session 5

This week we are headed into difficult territory that can leave many of us feeling vulnerable. This is also the point in our study when people may be comfortable enough with each other that they start accidentally trying to control one another—offering advice or overspiritualizing another person's process.

Be sure to redirect the conversation if anyone in the group tries to hit someone with well-meaning but unhelpful advice or begins asking detailed questions in an attempt to "fix" anyone's problems. When that happens, consider saying something like, "Suzy, it sounds like you have some great things to share. I'm sure if Greg hasn't tried that, he could follow up with you after group time if he would like. I would love to make sure we get to hear from everyone, so let's get back to the questions."

Session 5 Goal

To learn what reconciliation is and when it's possible; to discover how to regain trust

Welcome and Connection Question (10 minutes)

Ask these open-ended questions to start session 5 with your group:

> **As a kid, how did apologies work in your family? Was healthy conflict modeled between your parents or other adults in your home? What was your reaction when you got in trouble back then?**

Observations from Session 4 Daily Study (10 minutes)

Have each person share one or two things they are learning from their homework. Check in on whether they are making space at the end for quiet time.

Video Time (20 minutes)

Tune in to session 5: "Seek Restoration."

Reflection (10 minutes)

Consult session 5 in your guide for questions that follow the video content. You may not be able to answer every one in the time you have, so pick one or two to focus on and then return to this section if you have extra time.

In the Word (20 minutes)

> **How does your understanding of grace and forgiveness in Christ change the way you engage with reconciliation in your relationships? Is there a relationship in your life that you want to deepen or reconcile?**

Application (15 minutes)

Review the application question about the way each person wants to commit to grow in relationships. It can be easy for someone to say, "I want to grow in all of these!" but generally when our goals are too lofty, we forget or get discouraged before we can meet them. You may want to direct your group to think of one "effort" they want to make, perhaps even in only one relationship, as a focus for their application.

Prayer (5 minutes)

Consider breaking into pairs to pray specifically for the Spirit's work in what has been shared. Remember, it is God who transforms our hearts (Romans 12:1-2). Our job is to keep in step with the Spirit as He does the work!

😃 Session 6

This is an important session for you, as the leader, to allow pain or unresolved struggle within the group to be acceptable—even expected. The question we can ask one another is, "How are you experiencing God through this struggle?" because He always wants to meet us in these places!

Session 6 Goal
To answer the question "What if a relationship can't get better?"; to accept and understand how to experience forgiveness without reconciliation

Welcome and Connection Question (10 minutes)
Here's a possible question to get your group started:

> Share about one of your favorite places on earth. Describe the environment, the people, and the experiences you have when you are in that place. Now think back to last week's day 5 Meditation Moment. Share the "pleasant places" of blessing (whether relationships, opportunities, or insights) God has given you.

Observations from Session 5 Daily Study (10 minutes)

> Have you ever felt compelled to live by other people's standards? What is your general response to feeling controlled, influenced, or manipulated by other people's judgments?

Video Time (20 minutes)
Tune in to session 6: "An Invitation to Integrity."

Reflection (10 minutes)
Consult session 6 in your guide for questions that follow the video content. Since this might be your last session, look for high-level themes and learning that you can encourage in each person in your group.

In the Word (20 minutes)
In this last section of our study, we are focusing on aligning our intentions with our actions. You may want to spend some time discussing the question "Why do you sometimes *not* do what you say you will do?"

Application (15 minutes)

We close our time today returning to the fifth law of miracles: *Hope makes change possible.* In light of this, ask your group to reflect on how they have experienced God through this study. Where has He restored their hope? What *small is big* changes have they experienced in themselves? What miracles are they hoping for in their lives? If there is time, take a moment to record some of the experiences group members have had as evidence of the Spirit's work. If you've noticed some of these changes in others, be sure to share your observations with them as a specific gift of encouragement at the end of your time together.

Prayer (5 minutes)

Hebrews 12:1 says, "Let us throw off everything that hinders." As you close your time together, take a few minutes to pray for anyone who needs healing from an unreconciled relationship. Ask God to give them the power to forgive and the conviction to remain obedient to His direction and call in their lives.

Notes

A WORD OF WELCOME

1. Matthew 11:29, msg.
2. See Romans 8:1.
3. Dean Burnett, "What Happens in Your Brain When You Make a Memory?," *Guardian*, September 16, 2015, https://www.theguardian.com/education/2015/sep/16/what-happens-in-your-brain-when-you-make-a-memory.
4. John 13:34.

SESSION 1: SETTING UP FOR A MIRACLE

1. Dallas Willard, *Renovation of the Heart: Putting on the Character of Christ* (Colorado Springs, CO: NavPress, 2002), 49.
2. Brendon Manning, *The Ragamuffin Gospel: Good News for the Bedraggled, Beat-Up, and Burnt Out* (Portland, OR: Multnomah, 1999), 125.

SESSION 2: THE HEART OF THE MATTER

1. For more on how your temperament impacts your decision-making and relationships, you can access a free assessment using the Myers-Briggs Type Indicator at 16personalities.com.
2. See *The Miracle Moment*, page 37. Definition adapted from Edwin Friedman, *A Failure of Nerve: Leadership in the Age of the Quick Fix* (New York: Seabury Books, 2007), 151.
3. Richard J. Davidson et al., "Alterations in Brain and Immune Function Produced by Mindfulness Meditation," *Psychosomatic Medicine* 65, no. 4 (July 2003): 564–70, https://doi.org/10.1097/01.PSY.0000077505.67574.E3.
4. Bruce K. Waltke, *The Book of Proverbs, Chapters 1–15*, The New International Commentary on the Old Testament (Grand Rapids, MI: Eerdmans, 2004), 91.
5. Waltke, *Book of Proverbs*.

SESSION 3: HUMILITY IN ACTION

1. Andrew Murray, *Humility: The Journey toward Holiness* (Bloomington, MN: Bethany House, 2001), 10.

2. Frederick Dale Bruner, *The Gospel of John: A Commentary* (Grand Rapids, MI: Eerdmans, 2012), 156.
3. Bruner, *Gospel of John.*

SESSION 4: NO FEAR IN LOVE
1. Adapted from Karl Albrecht, "The (Only) 5 Fears We All Share," *Psychology Today*, March 22, 2012, https://www.psychologytoday.com/gb/blog/brainsnacks /201203/the-only-5-fears-we-all-share.
2. See text note on John 18:29, *English Standard Version Study Bible* (Wheaton, IL: Crossway, 2008), 2063.
3. Henri Nouwen, *The Return of the Prodigal Son: Anniversary Edition* (New York: Convergent, 2016), 48–49.

SESSION 5: SEEK RESTORATION
1. *NIV Hebrew-Greek Key Word Study Bible*, entry 3356 "metanoeo."

SESSION 6: AN INVITATION TO INTEGRITY
1. Adapted from Edwin Friedman, *A Failure of Nerve: Leadership in the Age of the Quick Fix* (New York: Seabury Books, 2007), 151.

About the Author

NICOLE UNICE is a pastor, counselor, and leadership coach who facilitates environments of safety and vulnerability so that leaders and teams can courageously identify obstacles keeping them from maximum potential. Her expertise in both individual and systems health and her skill as a coach and facilitator equip her to help organizations identify their actual problems and discover innovative solutions.

Nicole encourages her clients to work toward understanding themselves in order to effectively lead others. She employs a broad range of approaches from both counseling and leadership development, and is known for facilitating innovative thinking that brings individuals and teams to breakthrough insights. Working with Nicole, leaders can expect to be both inspired and challenged to think deeper and work harder to achieve their preferred outcomes.

As a sought-after speaker on stages of all sizes, Nicole has a down-to-earth style that allows even the largest gathering to feel conversational. Nicole is the author of several books focused on spiritual transformation and is a featured speaker through RightNow Media and Punchline. She is the host of the *Let's Be Real* podcast, a conversation about healthy relationships with ourselves and one another.

She holds degrees from the College of William and Mary and from Gordon-Conwell Theological Seminary.

Nicole and her husband, Dave, live in Richmond, Virginia, with their three children and two pups. Discover more at nicoleunice.com.

It's time to transform your relationships at home, in love, and at work.
Are you ready for your miracle moment?

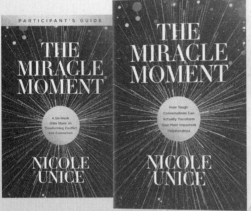

The Miracle Moment Discover the moment in every conversation that can change the whole relationship. Popular speaker Nicole Unice helps you discover the practical tools, words, and boundaries that will transform conflict into connection—even when you're tempted to shut up, blow up, or give up.

The Miracle Moment DVD Experience Nicole shines on video in this six-session series, teaching you how to recognize and respond to miracle moments and transform the relationships you have into the ones you really want.
Also available through online streaming at www.rightnowmedia.org.

The Miracle Moment Participant's Guide A six-session workbook designed to accompany *The Miracle Moment DVD Experience*, created for group or individual use.

Visit Nicole online at nicoleunice.com.

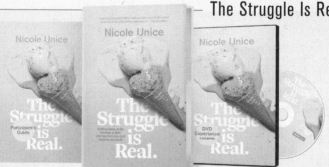